The Best Slow Cooker Recipes & Meals Cookbook

Over 100 Healthy Slow Cooker Recipes, Vegetarian Slow Cooker Recipes, Slow Cooker Chicken, Pot Roast Recipes, Beef Stew, Beef Bourguignon, Beef Stroganoff, Slow Cooker Soups, Chili Recipes, Breakfast Casserole Recipes, Slow Cooker Desserts and more!

By C Elias

Contents

Introduction

Today most families rely on instant or ready-made food because there seems to be no time to prepare and cook home-made food. Parents are working overtime, school children are busy with school assignments, school activities and so on. Everyone just grabs what they can!

But all of us would love to eat home-cooked food, and we wish we could have time to prepare it. This is where the 'slow cooker' comes in. We can still have that delicious, home-cooked meal. And the good news is, we don't have to watch it or stand over a stove while it is cooking because it will cook on its own.

A "slow cooker" is a counter-top domestic device which has a component that provides heat. It's a heat proof dish enclosed in a case (the cooker) with a glass lid. It is designed in such a way that food is cooked using slow and moist heat. Although the name Crock-Pot™ is a brand of a slow cooker, homemakers usually call any slow cooker a Crock-Pot™.

There are slow cookers that are also designed for a stove or an oven. The recipes in this book can be used for any slow cooking pot.

The advantages of cooking with a slow cooker

Why would anyone want to cook slowly at a low temperature slowly?

Firstly, it saves energy. You need less power to run a slow cooker and this means saving money. The kitchen will obviously stay cool because the slow cooker will not emit as much heat as an oven.

Your kitchen will have a cooler atmosphere because there is less heat coming out from the stove or the oven.

Tough meat cooks well slowly because during cooking the meat tissues separate from each other, and the collagen breaks down, resulting in a juicy and tender meat.

You get all the nutritional benefits of meat and vegetables when it is cooked under low temperature.

Preparing the ingredients is mostly simple and quick. You gather everything in the evening or even just a few minutes before going to work or out of the house and put them all in the cooker. When you are about to leave, just turn on the "slow cooker." When you come home, you have a delicious meal.

You don't have to worry about cleaning lots of pots and pans – just the one pot for the whole meal...!

Considerations for buying a Slow Cooker

Slow cookers come in different sizes. You must buy one that is sufficient for your family needs. A 3.5 litre "slow cooker" with cooking volume capacity of 2 litres, can cook food enough for two to four persons, while a 6 litre, with cooking volume capacity of 4.5 litres is good for six to eight persons.

You must also consider the shape of the "slow cooker." A round one is good for cooking stews or curries while an oval shaped "slow cooker" is good for cooking joints or whole chicken and other poultry.

Check the housing unit of the "slow cooker". Be sure the base is sturdy and there is sufficient flow of air at the bottom and space for heat to dispel. As full crocks are usually heavy make sure the handles are solid and sturdy. Consider also one that can withstand bumps as this will usually happen when you transfer it from the housing unit to the fridge, or while serving, washing or storing it.

Choose a removable crock so that you can easily clean it or place it in the refrigerator for future use. A removable crock can also be used as a serving dish. You don't need to transfer your food to another serving dish. Put the crock on the table, and anyone can serve himself or herself from it.

A "slow cooker" with a glass lid is a better option because you can see how the food is cooking. It is also good to consider one that has a higher doomed lid because it gives more room for cooking taller foods, like joints or whole poultry.

Another thing to consider in buying a slow cooker is it temperature settings. Some have one high and low settings while others have five settings ranging from as high as two hours to as slow as ten hours.

Generally, the heating capacity of slow cookers is as high as 160C/300°F, but the food never reaches a boiling point of 100C/212F, that is why the food can be left to cook for a longer period without being burned. The low cooking temperature allows the cooking to be left unattended. And even if the food is left longer than it was meant to be, it still does not overcook.

Another feature of a slow cooker is the warm setting, which allows the food that has already been cooked to stay warm while the side dishes are still being prepared.

More importantly, it is always best to test the slow cooker to see if everything is working well and to test how it can cook the food quickly on different settings. Don't use a party to test it. Try cooking a regular family meal.

More details and specifics on features and settings:

The auto cook is a feature that starts the slow cooker on high setting and turns to slow after an hour. Not all models have this feature, but most cooks believe this particular setting gives the best results.

When cooking cheaper cuts of red meats, the low setting is

preferable. This will vary from 8 to 12 hours.

High setting is recommended when cooking white meats like chicken. The setting here varies between 3 to 6 hours using slightly higher temperature.

When you need to cook faster without compromising the benefits of a low setting, you can turn the slow cooker to medium setting. Not all models have this feature.

The "keep warm" setting is for keeping the food warm without drying up or getting cold.

Some models come with timers that will automatically turn the setting after the meals is cooked to 'keep warm'. So if you are a working mother, choose one that has a timer.

Essential tips for using a slow cooker

Be watchful of the liquid when you are cooking in the slow cooker. Put enough liquid at the bottom of the cooker to prevent it from burning. The meat juice mixed with other liquid will produce stock.

The slow cooker must always be half-full of its maximum cooking potential. More food in the cooker slows down cooking time. Check if you have the correct heat settings so that it will not over-cook and dry out. If you are not too careful of your settings, what you intended to cook in eight hours, is cooked only in two and for six hours they are over-cooked and dried up.

For most people who are too busy to prepare dinner, meat is the usual food to cook in a slow cooker. Make sure that the meat to be cooked in the slow cooker is drained. Since it takes a longer time to cook meat, they should be placed on the bottom layer. This will also keep the meat moist as there is liquid underneath it.

Meats must be cooked for at least three hours in order to reach an internal temperature that will cook it properly.

If you want to cook vegetables in the slow cooker, you can toss in the tough and fibrous ones, like potatoes and carrots with the meat. These fibrous vegetables take longer to cook. Tomatoes, peppers, and mushrooms and other more delicate vegetables can be added half an hour before the meal is done.

It is best to try cooking various dishes to see how long your slow cooker can cook a particular meal.

You also have to try how to layer your food correctly and testing different heat settings in order for you to learn how to cook your meal best.

Must-have ingredients for a slow cooker

Here are some tips on how to make your dishes more delicious, if you have some staples available in your pantry.

Most pantries store different kinds of beans. When cooked well, they are the cheapest source of protein. Each kind has its own flavor especially when cooked with the right spices. Some people use it as their meal base when meat is not available or if they are vegetarian. Whatever kind of bean is used it won't matter as they all will produce a great meal in the slow cooker.

Most households have some potatoes stored away and they are very versatile...you can mash them, fry them, mix them with meat and other vegetables. In the slow cooker, it will thicken the soup, stews and other meat dishes. Because it is fibrous, it takes longer to cook so it should be thrown in with the meat in the slow cooker and allowed to cook all day.

Keep a stock of frozen vegetables as well then you can throw some in the pot at short notice.

Herbs can add more flavor to almost any kind of meal. Fresh herbs give more flavor than the dried ones. You can grow them in your backyard, as long as it gets enough sunlight, the soil is fertile and gets to be watered every day. You can dry the leaves if you want to store it. For slow cooker cooking, herbs must be added when cooking is almost finished so that its flavor will evenly get into the cooked meal.
Keep some broth cubes handy. When cooking in a slow

cooker, it is necessary to have sufficient liquid at the bottom of the pot. You can use broth or water. Cheap broth is available in almost all grocery stores, and they come in different kinds – chicken, pork, beef and vegetables. Some are already seasoned and so it is easy to add flavor to your meat dishes. Best to use organic though of course if you can find it.

Flour or cornstarch are basic ingredients to thicken a dish. You can powder your meat slightly with flour and sauté it in olive oil before putting it in the slow cooker to get a thicker sauce. Adding cornstarch to the remaining liquid can serve as creamy gravy.

Remember that flour is used as a thickener while cornstarch is for smooth gravy.

Although meat is not a pantry staple, considering that it is the main ingredient of most slow cooker meals, it is best that you have some in the freezer, available when you need it. When cooked in a slow cooker, a tougher cut of meat gets enough moisture and becomes tender, making it melt in your mouth, unlike when cooked in the oven where it becomes tough and dried up.

With some of these ingredients within hand's reach, you will be able to prepare dinner without much effort. Create new recipes by combining any or all of what is in your pantry.

Enjoy cooking with a slow cooker!

Planning a meal

First of all, it is necessary that you have a main ingredient. The best main ingredient is either meat or beans. Although some people use grains as their main base, it is not advisable to use the slow cooker to cook grains because they cook very quickly and comes out mushy when overcooked. Pastas are cooked best when boiled.

Choose a base that can withstand the period of time required for slow cooker cooking and the temperature. Pork, beef and almost all kinds of poultry are good meat base. Most beans can also withstand the heating process of a slow cooker. Having chosen your main ingredient, make sure you wash it before using it. Always remember to add a little liquid at the bottom.

Next, you have to choose what to add to the base. Most types of meat base cook well with any kind of vegetable. If you have some baby carrots put them on top of your meat or bean base.

While still planning what ingredients to add to your meal, start the cooker. If you have red-skinned potatoes, wash them very well and add them to the cooker. You don't have to slice or dice them.

If there is celery and some onion in your refrigerator, place them in the skillet, add salt, pepper and cooking wine and cook them until the wine has reduced and the vegetables are cooked.

Now, your main ingredient needs seasoning or spices. Why not include some cilantro (coriander), turmeric or cumin? To get some Indian flavor, add curry. To make it taste like an Italian dish, a dash of basil, oregano bay leaf, rosemary or coriander (cilantro) will do the job. Remember that fresh herbs give a better taste. Use the powdered spices if fresh ones are not available.

An hour or so before the end of the cooking time you can put in the vegetables and spices you have sautéed. Stir and savor the smell of the delicious flavor of your meal. If you find that the amount of liquid is more than what you desire, remove the lid and turn the cooker to high setting. It enhances evaporation of the excess liquid leaving you with the desired amount of broth, and then you can turn it to low.

Of course, the above recommendations require you to be near the slow cooker about an hour or so before the meal is required. But you can just as easily throw everything in, leave and eat when you return.

Some tips on slow cooked soups and stews

The slow cooker was designed mainly for soups and stews. Soups are everyone's favorite. They are easy to make. There are thin soups, like chicken noodle or some Thai soups. There are also thick soups like vichyssoise or borscht, a Ukrainian soup usually made with beets and starchy vegetables which represents ethnic soup dishes.

Thicker soups sustain you between meals. Together with a slice of bread, you have a complete meal.

You need more liquid than a regular meal to make a soup in a slow cooker. Just add two or three more cups of broth or water to your cooker. If your slow cooker is large, put in more liquid, taking into consideration the other ingredients you would also want to add.

If you are using meat, put it in first. Cubed raw chicken are best for soups. Buy cubed beef for stew so you won't have to cube them yourself. Frozen meat should be thawed first before adding it to the slow cooker. Before adding the meat in the cooker, you can also cook the meat in a pan until it turns crusty but the insides are still uncooked. This is called searing. This method increases the flavor of the meat in the soup.

Once the meat is in the cooker, you can now add your vegetables to the soup. Chop into soup-sized pieces your potatoes, carrots, squash, zucchini, and onions. Celery is usually used as a vegetable for soups. To retain its firm texture wait a couple of hours before the end of cooking before adding it in. Even frozen veggies can be added to the soup. Allow your soup mixture to cook for about six to eight hours.

For slow cooker meals, a creamier soup is preferable. Heavy cream won't scorch even with longer cooking time. If milk is required, it is best to use evaporated milk because its liquid component has been taken out. It also gives a creamier texture, and it does not curdle like the other kinds of milk.

Now for the finishing touches. When cheese is required, add it to your potato soup or chowders when it is almost done. Sprinkle some rosemary, dill, basil, oregano, or parsley on top. You can even add chives, leeks, shallots, and garlic to enhance the flavor of your soups and stews. You can also garnish it with chives, parsley, or leeks.

Doesn't that sound delicious? One good thing about soup is that it can be frozen in bowls and then thawed when you need it. You can keep your soup in the freezer and use it as liquid for your other slow cooker recipes.

Tips for healthy slow cooker meals

Most recipes require that you add a little sugar for sweetness. However, studies will show that sugar is the worst kind of food. Too much sugar in our body will drive our insulin levels crazy. Insulin is released by your pancreas in order to normalize our blood sugar levels. 'Insulin resistance' in the cells of the body develops when a person is always eating sugar. Obesity, body malaise, high blood pressure, certain heart diseases, diabetes, dementia, Alzheimer's and several cancers are diseases attributed to insulin resistance.

Avoid artificial sweeteners as well as they have been proven to cause health problems (check the net!).

If you need to sweeten a dish I recommend you use xylitol. This is a natural sweetener found in almost all local health shops. It is the sugar found in fruits, vegetables, and birch and hardwood trees. It is anti-bacterial, low in GI and will not cause fluctuations in the blood sugar level. However, it is not recommended for pets as it will have a different effect on them and cause serious problems.

Stevia powder or liquid is also a good alternative. Stevia is a very sweet herb used in South America for the past 1500 years. It is proven that it does not contain calories. In fact it is said that it is the best sweetener in the market today.

Pork is considered as dirty meat because pigs eat anything, and they are carrier of parasites and certain viruses which are difficult to kill when even the meat is cooked. More people get sick eating dirty pork. Even organic pork is not safe to eat. You will notice that pigs don't sweat and they digest food so quickly, so that toxins are not flushed out of their bodies.

But the choice of the reader prevails. So although I have not included any pork recipes in this book – you can use it in some of the recipes instead of other meat.

Lastly when using meat, choose the organic or grass-fed beef if you can afford to... It tastes much better and lacks toxins and chemicals.

Sauces

Some of the recipes included in this article will require for ready-made sauces and soup packs. It is recommended to try and look for organic ones and if possible without sugar or additives. Of course it is best to make your own sauces, soups or broths as suggested before. You can also use other ingredients like tomato puree instead of a sauce or tinned tomatoes.

Below are 2 quick soups you can make and freeze or use straight away in some of the slow cooker recipes.

Quick Cream of Mushroom Soup:
All you need to do is saute mushrooms in a pan using little oil or butter, add in some chicken broth (made with a stock cube or made from slow cooking a left over chicken carcas) add some flour to thicken, then any milk of choice (coconut, almond or dairy), thyme and more salt and pepper. You can even add a little sherry. For a smooth soup puree the mushrooms and chicken broth before adding the milk and flour etc. Vary the quantities of the above according to taste, numbers of guests etc.

Quick Cream of Chicken Soup:
There are many ways to make this but here are some ideas. Fry some onion and garlic or cook in a little chicken stock until soft. Add a jug of chicken stock, salt, pepper, parsley and any other seasoning. Add milk of choice and flour to make creamy. Add cooked meat if desired and then blend in a processor. You can add cooked carrot, leek and potatoe as well for more flavor and thickness.

Slow Cooker Chicken

SWEET CHICKEN SQUASH

Ingredients:

2 pieces big chicken breasts
1 piece acorn squash
2 x parsnips
14.5 ounce chicken broth
Garlic chopped (you can add as much as you desire)
Nutmeg
Honey
Salt
Pepper

Cooking Directions:

Remove the peel from parsnips and then chop it. Place it first in the slow cooker.
Sprinkle with chopped garlic.
Put the chicken right on top.
Add the chicken broth.
Peel the skin off the squash and cut into chunks. Place the chunks of squash on top.
Season with nutmeg, salt and pepper.
Pour over honey until the squash is lightly covered. Cook this on moderate temperature for 8 hours.

CREAMY CHICKEN PASTA

Ingredients:

4 pieces chicken breasts skinned and bone removed
Half cup of margarine
11 ounce can of golden mushroom soup
1.05 ounce Italian salad dressing mix
Half cup of white wine
8 ounce angel hair pasta
4 ounce onion and chive cream cheese

Cooking Directions:

Use a saucepan to melt the margarine, use only low heat.
Pour in mushroom soup and some white wine.
Add the salad dressing and the onion and chive cream cheese.
Stir continuously to completely melt the cream cheese and the consistency is smooth.
Pour the sauce over the chicken.
Cook the chicken for six hours over low heat.
Prepare the pasta.
Once done, you can now serve the chicken over the pasta.

ITALIAN PEA AND CHICKEN

Ingredients:

4 pieces chicken breasts cut in half, skin and bones removed
Pinch of salt
Pinch of pepper
Pinch of Paprika
1 tbsp of oil
1 clove garlic, minced
1 onion, chopped
1 red pepper, chopped
Half teaspoon rosemary leaves (dried)
14.5 ounce can of crushed tomatoes
10 ounce of frozen peas

Cooking Directions:

Use salt, pepper and paprika to seasoned the chicken breasts.
Place a medium skillet over a medium heat.
Put oil and add chicken until brown.
Place the chicken in the crock-pot.
Combine the rest of the ingredients in a small bowl, except for the peas. Pour the mixture over the chicken.
Cover this and cook over low heat for 9 hours.
Just before serving it, add the peas.
Serve this over rice.
Makes 3 to 4 servings.

ARTICHOKE & MUSHROOM CHICKEN SURPRISE

Ingredients

One and a half chicken breasts, skinned and deboned
Two cups fresh mushrooms, sliced
14.5 ounce can tomatoes, diced
9 ounce package of frozen artichokes
One cup of chicken broth
One medium onion, chopped
¼ cup drained capers
¼ cup white wine (dry)
3 tbsp fast cooking tapioca
3 tsp curry powder
¾ tsp dried and crushed thyme
¼ tsp salt
¼ tsp pepper
4 cups of hot and cooked couscous

Cooking Directions:

First, rinse the chicken thoroughly and set aside.
Mix mushrooms, tomatoes, onion, olives, frozen artichokes, wine and chicken broth.
Add in salt, pepper, curry powder, tapioca and thyme. Place the chicken inside and use a spoon to help marinade the chicken with the tomato.
Set the cooker to low and cook the dish for 8 hours.
Serve the dish with hot and cooked couscous.
Makes 6 servings.

BOURBON CHICKEN PIECES

Ingredients

4 chicken breast cut in half
¼ cup of flour
½ tsp of paprika
Pinch of salt to taste
2 tbsp of butter
2 tbsp of oil
2 pieces of onions, chopped
2 tbsp of parsley, chopped
¼ tsp of chervil, dried
¼ cup of bourbon
4 ounce can of mushrooms
10 ounce can of tomatoes
¼ tsp of sugar
Salt and pepper to taste

Cooking Directions:

Combine flour, salt and paprika and let the chicken soak in mixture.
In a skillet, heat oil and butter. Sauté the chicken thoroughly on both sides until completely brown.
Add in onion, chervil and parsley and cook for a while and then remove from the heat. Put the chicken inside the slow cooker.
Mix all the rest of the ingredients and pour it over the chicken. Cook over low heat for 7 hours. Serve this over noodles or rice. Makes 4 servings

YAMMY CHICKEN CURRY

Ingredients:

2 lbs of chicken thighs and legs cut in chunks
Oil
3 big yams, skin removed and chopped
2 X white onions, chopped
1 tbsp garlic, minced
1 tbsp ginger, minced
1/3 cup curry powder
1 medium banana
2 x bay leaves
4 cups of chicken stock
Salt
Black pepper

Cooking Directions:

Coat a large saucepan with oil. Get the chicken and season it and then brown it on all sides. Put it aside. Get rid of all the fat on the pot and leave only the oil.
Sauté ginger, garlic and onions in the same pot. Put the curry powder.
Mix them for 2 minutes just make sure that the curry powder will not burn. Place it into slow cooker.
Place all chicken, banana, broth and the rest of the ingredients into the slow cooker and cook for 4 hours on low heat. Season to taste. Best served on basmati rice.

ALMOND & WHITE WINE CHICKEN

Ingredients

1 cup chicken, diced
2 onions, chopped
2 celery stalks, chopped
2 cups rice, cooked
¼ cup white wine, dry
2 cups chicken broth
1 cup almonds, sliced

Cooking Directions

Mix all the ingredients and place them inside the slow cooker. Cook it for 8 hours on low heat. Serve it with toasted sliced almonds.

Serve over rice.

CREAM CHEESE & BROCCOLI CHICKEN

Ingredients:

6 pieces chicken breasts, skinned, cubed and frozen
3 tbsp olive oil
1.05 ounce package of Italian dressing mix
11 ounce can of celery soup cream
8 ounce package of cream cheese, cut in cubes
¼ cup of chicken broth
1 gram chopped onions
Half cup sliced mushrooms, fresh
¼ tsp minced garlic
10 ounce package of broccoli florets, frozen

Cooking Directions:

Pour the olive oil in a medium bowl. Add the chicken cubes and cover it properly. Put the Italian dressing and the chicken inside a zip lock bag. Shake it to coat the chicken well. Put the chicken inside the slow cooker. Cover it tightly and cook in 3 ½ hours on low heat. Place an skillet over a medium heat. Heat the oil. Sauté onion and mushrooms. Add in the cream cheese, chicken broth and the soup. Put the garlic and stir until you get a smooth mixture. Seasoned with salt and pepper. Pour this mixture on the chicken, cover tightly and cook for another hour.

Tip – Frozen chicken won't dry up and cooks better if placed inside a slow cooker. Cut them in cubes before you freeze them to make it easier.

CHEDDAR CHICKEN DINNER

Ingredients:

6 pieces chicken breasts, skinned and deboned
Salt and Pepper
Garlic powder
2 cans chicken soup cream
1 can of cheddar cheese soup

Cooking Directions:

Wash the chicken thoroughly and season it with garlic powder, salt and pepper.
Combine the two soups and then pour it on the chicken inside the slow cooker.
Cook for 8 hours on low heat. Best serve with noodles or rice.

BURGUNDY CHICKEN & POTATO

Ingredients:

2 pieces chicken breast
1 clove garlic, crushed
¼ tbsp of pepper
2/3 cup of sliced green onions
8 pieces peeled white onions
8 pieces scrubbed new potatoes
1 tsp salt
1 cup of chicken broth
1 cup of burgundy wine
½ tsp thyme, dried
Parsley, chopped

Cooking Directions:

In a skillet, heat oil, sauté green onions and then remove them and let them drain on a paper towel. Place the chicken to skillet and let them turn into brown on all sides. When it turned brown, remove and set it aside.
In a slow cooker, place mushrooms, garlic and onions.
Add in the chicken salt, pepper, potatoes, thyme, green onions and the broth.
Cover tightly and cook for 8 hours on low heat. In the last hour, add in the Burgundy and cook on high heat.
Serve with garnish.

TOMATO & MUSHROOM CHICKEN

Ingredients:

Pieces of chicken
A can of tomatoes, chopped
1 piece onion, chopped
1 piece green pepper, chopped
1 piece garlic clove, minced
1 tbsp Italian herbs
Pepper flakes
Mushrooms and black olives

Cooking Directions:

Put the chicken inside a slow cooker, add tomatoes and the remaining ingredients.
Cook in 8 hours on low heat.
In the last hour add in the olives. Sprinkle with parmesan cheese and pepper flakes.
Best serve over pasta.

SWEET SHERRY CHICKEN

Ingredients:

2 pounds of chicken tenders, boneless
1 cup of carrot cut into matchstick
1 cup of cheese spread and olive
A bunch of green onions, sliced
2 tbsp sherry, dried
A can of cream of chicken soup, fat-free
Salt and Pepper

Cooking Directions:

Place everything inside the slow cooker based on the order given above.
Stir them just to combine everything properly.
Cover tightly and cook for 9 hours over low heat.
Best serve with rice, toast or biscuits. Makes 8 servings.

OLIVE AND CHEESE SPREAD RECIPE

Ingredients:

1 cup cream cheese, non-fat; Half tsp of Basil, dried
¼ tsp of garlic powder; 15 pieces of minced black olives
¼ cup diced pimientos
1 tbsp of fresh chives, minced

Cooking Directions:

Just combine all the seasonings with cream cheese and add in pimientos and olives.

CHICKEN NOODLE CASSEROLE

Ingredients:

8 ounce package noodles
3 cups cooked chicken, diced
½ cup celery, diced
½ cup green pepper, diced
½ cup onion, diced
4 ounce of canned mushrooms
4 ounce of canned pimiento
½ cup of parmesan cheese
1 ½ cups of cottage cheese in cream style
1 cup cheese, grated
1 can of chicken soup cream
½ cup of chicken broth
½ tsp of fresh basil
2 tbsp of butter, melted

Cooking Directions:

Cook the noodles according to package directions.
Rinse and drain well. Using a separate bowl, combine all
the rest of the ingredients with the noodles.
Grease the slow cooker and place the mixture inside.
Cover it with the lid and cook for 8 hours over low heat.
Makes 6 servings.

POTATO CHICKEN CASSEROLE

Ingredients:

3 cups cooked chicken, diced
2 cans of chicken broth
½ tsp salt
½ tsp pepper
1 stalk of celery sliced thinly
1 onion, chopped
1 piece of bay leaf
3 cups of peeled and cubed potatoes
1 package of mixed veggies, frozen
1 cup of milk
1 cup plain flour
1 tsp of pepper
½ tsp salt
9 inch frozen pie crust

Cooking Directions:

Mix chicken, salt, pepper, onion, potatoes, mixed veggies, celery, bay leaf and broth in a slow cooker. Cover properly and cook for 10 hours on low heat. Take the bay leaf out and pre-heat your oven to 400 degree F. In a bowl, mix flour and milk together. Mix flour with water and pour it slowly into the slow cooker. Add the pepper, salt and poultry seasoning. Take out the liner and put the 9-inch pie crust on the mixture. Put the liner in the preheated oven and bake it without cover for 15 minutes. If you do not have a removable liner, just place the mixture in a casserole dish. Cover it using the pie crust and bake it. Makes 8 servings.

CHILI CHICKEN DINNER

Ingredients

3 chicken breasts, cut into pieces
1 cup onion, chopped
1 cup bell pepper, chopped
2 cloves garlic
2 tbsp vegetable oil
2 cans stewed tomatoes, Mexican style
1 can chili beans
2/3 cup picante sauce
1 tsp chili powder
1 tsp cumin powder
½ tsp salt

Cooking Directions;

Use a skillet to sauté garlic, onion, pepper and chicken in vegetable oil. Move them to slow cooker and stir in the rest of the ingredients.
Cook this for 6 hours on low heat. Best serve with rice.
Makes 6 servings.

PICANTE SAUCE

Ingredients

1 can of tomato puree
1 tbsp white vinegar
1/3 cup finely chopped onion
3 finely chopped Jalapeño peppers

½ tsp salt
1 ¼ cup water

Cooking Directions;

Combine all the ingredients together and cook on a medium heat. Bring this to a boil. Lower the heat and let it simmer until it becomes thick. Once thick, remove from heat and let it cool. Put it in the jar.

SIMPLE CHICKEN SOUP

Ingredients:

2 chopped onions
3 sliced carrots
2 sliced celery stalks
2 tsp salt
¼ tsp pepper
½ tsp basil
¼ tsp thyme
3 tbsp parsley, in flakes
1 package peas, frozen
3 lb of chicken meat
4 cups chicken stock
1 cup of noodles

Cooking Directions:

Place all the ingredients inside a slow cooker, but set aside the noodles. Cover tightly and cook for 10 hours on low heat.
An hour before serving, take away the chicken and let it cool. Get the meat from the bones and place meat again to slow cooker.
Stir in noodles. Bring the heat to high.
Cook it again for another hour.

TURKEY WITH CRANBERRY & APPLE

Ingredients:

2 tsp margarine or melted butter
½ cup of chicken broth
1 big apple, chopped
½ cup onion, chopped
1 chopped celery stalk
1 cup cranberry sauce
¾ tsp poultry seasoning
2 cups of seasoned crumb
2 pounds of turkey, breast part - in cutlets

Cooking Directions:

Mix chicken broth with onion, celery, apple, chicken broth, butter, cranberry sauce, stuffing and poultry seasoning. Add 3 tablespoon of stuffing mix on each cutlet of turkey. Roll each cutlet and tie it up.
Cook in pot for 4 hours on low heat.

COUNTRY CAPTAIN CHICKEN BREASTS

Ingredients:

2 x apples
1 onion, chopped
1 green bell pepper, chopped
3 cloves minced garlic
2 tbsp currants, dried
1 tbsp curry powder
1 tsp ginger
¼ tsp red pepper
1 can tomatoes, diced
6 chicken breasts cut in halves, skinned and bones removed
½ cup chicken broth
1 cup white rice
1/3 cup almonds
Parsley, chopped
Salt

Cooking Directions:

In a slow cooker, place apples, bell pepper, garlic, onion, curry powder, currants, red pepper and ginger.
Add in the tomatoes.
Wash the chicken and dry.
Arrange the ingredients in overlapping manner.
Add in the broth.
Cook for 7 hours over low heat.
Place the chicken on overproof plate and place in a 200 degree oven to keep it warm.
Add rice to cooking liquid and cook in high heat.
Cover tightly and stir twice until the rice is tender.

Use a nonstick frying pan for toasting almonds and then set aside.
Season rice with salt.
Place in a serving dish and put the chicken on top.
Sprinkle almonds and parsley on top.

CREAMY MUSHROOM CHICKEN WITH RICE

Ingredients:

Chicken breasts
Cream of mushroom soup
1 tbsp olive oil
Onion soup mix
Brown rice with long grain
1 tbsp thyme, crushed
Salt
Pepper
Broccoli florets
Red pepper, diced

Cooking Directions:

In cooking brown rice, you have to add 2 ¼ cups of liquid for each cup of rice.
Place the content of soup in a measuring cup.
In a pan, pour olive oil and add the rice until it starts to crackle.
This rice will become dense and retain its shape when cooking.
Add the soups, herbs, seasonings and extra water.
Mix all the ingredients in slow cooker except for the veggies.
Cook for 10 hours on low heat.
Add veggies during the last 45 minutes.
his recipe is great with fresh salad and crusty bread.

SAUCY CHICKEN

Ingredients:

4 chicken breasts cut into pieces
2 tbsp butter, melted
Salt and pepper
1 package Italian seasoning mix, dry
1 can chicken soup cream
8 ounce of cubed cream cheese
½ cup of chicken broth
1 big onion
1 garlic, crushed

Cooking Directions:

Season chicken with butter and sprinkle it with Italian seasoning mix.
Cover tightly and cook for 7 hours on low heat.
During the last 45 minutes, sauté onion in butter and add in cream cheese, chicken broth and soup.
Add the garlic and the rest of the ingredients until it becomes smooth. Seasoned with salt and pepper.
Pour the mixture on chicken in slow cooker and cook for another 45 minutes.
Remove the chicken and place it in a platter.
Make sure that you stir the sauce before pouring it over the chicken.

DUSK CHICKEN DINNER

Ingredients

4 lbs chicken cut in cubes
1 chopped onion
2 cloves garlic, chopped
1 chopped green pepper
1 peeled and chopped tomato
1 cup white wine, dry
A pinch of cayenne pepper

Cooking Directions:

Mix all the ingredients in the slow cooker.
Cover and then cook for 8 hours on low heat.
You may also cook this for 5 ½ hours and then put the chicken over cookie sheets and cook again for 45 minutes at 350 degree to make the skin crispy.
Serve this with French bread.
Makes 5 servings.

CARROTS & CHICKEN STEW

Ingredients:

Chicken breasts, skinned and bones removed
1 medium cabbage, quartered
1 lb carrots cut into cubes
Potatoes cubed
Water
4 chicken bouillon cubes
1 tsp poultry seasoning
¼ tsp seasoning, Greek style
2 tbsp cornstarch
¼ cup of water

Cooking Directions:

Wash chicken thoroughly and put it in a slow cooker.
Wash cabbage and put it on top of chicken and then add in carrots.
Put just enough water to cover almost all of them inside.
Add chicken bouillon cubes and sprinkle poultry seasoning.
Add in Greek seasoning.
Cook for 8 hours on low heat.

For Gravy - when you are ready to eat, pour a little amount of the juice in a saucepan. Let this boil. Mix cornstarch or flour in a ¼ cup of water. Pour this to the saucepan and let it simmer until it becomes thick. You can pour the gravy over chicken and potatoes.

CHICKEN & PEA CREAM STEW

Ingredients:

1 can of chicken soup cream (or make your own)
3 tbsp of flour
¼ tsp pepper
A dash of cayenne pepper
1 pound of chicken breasts, cut in cubes
1 celery, chopped
½ cup green pepper, chopped
¼ cup chopped onion
1 package frozen peas, thawed
2 tbsp pimientos, drained and diced
Cooked rice

Cooking Directions:

Mix flour, peppers and soup in a slow cooker and stir until it becomes smooth.
Add in chicken, onion, celery and green pepper.
Cover and then cook for 8 hours on low heat. Add in pimientos and peas.
Cook for another 30 minutes. Best serve with rice.

SPANISH CHICKEN & TURKEY SAUSAGE

Ingredients:

3 pounds chicken meat in pieces
1 tbsp of cooking oil
8 ounce of cooked and smoked turkey sausage, sliced
1 onion, sliced
3 minced garlic cloves
2 tbsp fresh thyme
¼ tsp of black pepper
1/8 tsp saffron
1 cup of chicken broth
½ cup of water
2 cups tomatoes, chopped
2 yellow sweet peppers, cut into strips
1 cup of green peas, frozen
3 cups of hot cooked rice

Cooking Directions:

Skin and wash the chicken thoroughly.
In a large pan, brown the pieces of chicken in hot oil.
Drain the fat and put the chicken in slow cooker.
Add in onion and turkey sausage. Sprinkle it with thyme, saffron, garlic, black pepper and turmeric.
Add in water and broth.
Cover and cook for 8 hours on low heat.
Serve with hot rice.

CHICKEN CACCIATORE WITH WINE

Ingredients:

1 big onion, sliced thinly
1 ½ pound of chicken breasts, skinned and deboned
2 cans of tomato paste
8 ounce of fresh mushrooms, sliced
½ tsp salt
¼ tsp pepper
2 minced garlic cloves
1 tsp oregano
1 bay leaf
½ tsp basil
¼ cup of water
¼ cup of white wine, dry

Cooking Directions:

Place the sliced onion at the bottom of slow cooker. Place the pieces of chicken. Add in mushrooms, herbs, tomato paste, salt, pepper, water and white wine. Spread this over chicken. Cover and cook for 9 hours over low heat. Serve the pieces of chicken over vermicelli or hot spaghetti. Makes 4 servings.

SWISS CHICKEN DELIGHT

Ingredients:

6 chicken breasts, pounded until thin
6 Swiss cheese, sliced
Ham slices
1 can of cream of mushroom soup
Flour, milk and broth
¼ cup milk
Salt and pepper

Cooking Directions:

Wrap the cheese all over the chicken. If you are using ham, wrap it first and then roll up and use a toothpick to secure it. Put the chicken in slow cooker and place the rest of the ingredients on top. Combine milk and soup and pour this over the chicken. Cover and cook for 4 hours on low heat. Best serve with noodles.

CHICKEN NOODLE SOUP

Ingredients:

3 carrots, peel removed and cut into chunks
3 celery stalks cut into chunks
1 big quartered onion
3 chicken breasts, skinless and cut in halves
2 cans of fat-free chicken broth
3 cups of water
Dried dill
Dried parsley
8 ounce of noodles

Cooking Directions

Place the vegetables inside the slow cooker. Add the chicken in and pour water and broth. Add parsley and dill. Cover and cook for 8 hours on low heat. Remove chicken and veggies from slow cooker. Place the noodles and turn the heat to high while you mince veggies and shred chicken. You may also use food processor for the veggies. Place the veggies and chicken again in slow cooker and heat it again. It would take 20 minutes for the noodles to be cooked.

BRAISED CHICKEN IN RED WINE

Ingredients:

4 pound cut up roasted chicken
12 pieces peeled white onions
½ tsp salt
¼ tsp black pepper
¼ cup of cognac or brandy
2 peeled and crushed garlic cloves
¼ tsp ground thyme
1 bay leaf
1 ½ red wine, strong and dry
5 tbsp flour
1 cup of chicken bouillon cubes
¾ pound mushrooms, fresh, stemmed and wiped
1 tbsp margarine or butter
¼ tsp salt
1 tbsp fresh parsley, chopped

Cooking Directions:

Place the onions in slow cooker. Take away the fat and cut the chicken into diced pieces.
Heat fat in skillet on medium heat.
Remove the shriveled bits and sauté chicken until they become brown on all sides.
Seasoned with salt and pepper. Make the brandy warm with the help of a small saucepan or a ladle.
Use a match to warm the brandy and pour this quickly on top of chicken.
Once the flame died, lift the chicken and put it in slow

cooker. Add in garlic, bay leaf and thyme.

Pour wine in a hot skillet and get the juice out of the pan. Dissolve flour in the bouillon and pour this over the skillet. Simmer this and stir briskly to avoid lumps from forming. Pour this in slow cooker.

Cover and cook for 9 hours on low heat.

Just before serving, melt butter in skillet and sauté mushroom over medium heat.

The mushroom will become tender after five minutes.

Add in salt and then place the chicken casserole.

Let the sauce simmer until you get the right consistency. Garnish with parsley before serving.

DELUXE CHICKEN CACCIATORE

Ingredients:

5 pounds chicken, cut in pieces
1 cup of flour
¼ cup olive oil
1 cup onions, chopped
1 cup mushrooms, sliced
1 cup sliced carrots (cut lengthwise)
2 tbsp garlic, minced
8 cups tomatoes, peeled and chopped
¾ cup Marsala wine
½ cup of tomato paste
Romano cheese, grated freshly
1 tsp basil
1 tsp oregano
1 ½ tsp salt
1 tsp pepper

Cooking Instructions:

Rinse and drain chicken pieces thoroughly. Use a deep skillet and heat the oil.
Coat each piece of chicken in flour and fry until golden brown.
Bring the chicken pieces to paper towels and let them drain.
Sauté onion, carrots, mushroom, garlic and green pepper in the same skillet.
After 10 minutes, add in tomatoes and sauté for again for a few minutes.
Add in tomato paste, herbs, wine salt and pepper and cook

on medium heat.
After 5 minutes, add the pieces of chicken and mix thoroughly.
Bring all the ingredients in slow cooker and cook for 5 hours on low heat.
Best serve with noodles.
Sprinkle with grated cheese.

MEXICAN FIESTA CHICKEN

Ingredients:

3 pounds chicken breasts, skinned, bones removed and cut into pieces
2 tbsp oil
1 chopped onion
1 tsp oregano
1 jalapeno pepper, chopped finely
3 minced garlic cloves
1 can diced tomatoes, Mexican style
¼ tsp cumin

Cooking Directions:

In a skillet, heat the oil and cook the pieces of chicken until golden brown.
Remove the chicken and drain.
Add onion, garlic, jalapeno and green bell pepper in skillet.
Sauté the ingredients until they are slightly cooked.
Add these ingredients to slow cooker and mix well.
Cover and cook for 8 hours on low.
Best serve with flour tortillas.

GARLIC CHICKEN WITH CABBAGE

Ingredients:

A whole chicken
1 chopped white onion
1 cabbage
2 tbsp margarine or butter
8 cloves of garlic
Salt and pepper

Cooking Directions:

Season the chicken and put in slow cooker.
Add in garlic, onion, salt and pepper.
Fill it with water.
Cover and cook on for 8 hours on high.
You will know it is done once the chicken fall off its bone.
In the last cooking hour, cut the cabbage head.
Put a large pot pan and place one cup of water in it.
Add in butter and sprinkle it with salt, pepper and garlic.
Cover and cook for 30 minutes on medium heat.
When the chicken and cabbage are cooked, place cabbage in a bowl and put the chicken on top.
Pour the chicken broth over the chicken.
Add any seasonings that you prefer.

GREEK STYLE CHICKEN

Ingredients:

6 chicken breast, skinned
1 can of tomato puree
1 can of tomato sauce
1 can mushrooms, sliced
1 can olives, ripe
1 tbsp garlic
1 tbsp lemon juice
1 chopped onions
1 tsp oregano
½ cup brandy or wine
2 cups of rice
Salt

Cooking Directions:

Rinse and take away the fat from chicken.
Bake chicken in 350 degree oven for one hour.
Combine the remaining ingredients except rice.
Place the sauce and the chicken in slow cooker and cook for 4 hours over low heat.
Cook rice based on directions.
Serve the chicken over rice with its sauce.

HONEY CHICKEN

Ingredients:

8 skinless and boneless chicken thighs
½ tsp of salt
½ tsp of ginger
½ cup of honey
1 cup of dried fruit
¼ tsp of pepper
1/3 cup of chicken broth
1 onion, diced

Cooking Directions:

Place the thighs of chicken in the slow cooker.
Seasoned with salt, pepper and ginger, just make sure that the chicken is covered properly.
Spread dried fruit evenly on chicken.
Add in chicken broth and honey.
Put the onion next and cover.
Cook for 8 hours on low heat.

JERKY CHICKEN

Ingredients:

1 big onion, cut in pieces
1 tbsp chopped ginger
1 seeded and minced habanero pepper
½ tsp allspice, ground
2 tbsp dry mustard
1 tsp black pepper, freshly ground
2 tbsp balsamic vinegar or red wine
2 tbsp soy sauce
2 crushed and minced garlic cloves
4 pounds tenders of chicken

Cooking Directions:

Mix ginger and onion using a food processor.
Wait until they are chopped finely.
Add the rest of the ingredients, except for the chicken.
Make sure that everything are combined well.
Put the chicken in slow cooker and pour the sauce over.
Cover and cook for 8 hours on low heat.
Makes 4 servings.

LAZY SLOW CHICKEN

Ingredients

1 package chicken breasts without the bones
1 can mushroom soup cream
1 jar mushrooms, sliced
¼ cup of flour
Paprika, salt and pepper

Cooking Directions:

Wash chicken breasts thoroughly.
Seasoned with paprika, salt and pepper on all sides.
Put it in slow cooker.
Mix the rest of the ingredients and add them to slow cooker.
Cook this on low heat the whole day.
Best serve with rice, mashed potatoes or noodles.

LEMON & ROSEMARY CHICKEN

Ingredients:

2 pounds of chicken breasts, skinned and bones removed
1 tbsp vegetable oil
½ cup lemon juice
1 crushed garlic clove
1 tsp of dried rosemary
¼ tsp pepper
¼ tsp salt

Cooking Directions:

Get a food storage bag and put garlic, lemon juice, salt, pepper and rosemary.
Put the chicken and close the bag.
Let it marinate for 4 hours inside the refrigerator.
Make sure that you turn the bag from time to time.
Put the chicken in slow cooker and add the marinade on top.
Cover and cook until tender, occasionally basting with its marinade.
Add the frozen carrots and broccoli one hour before it is cooked.
Makes 6 servings.

LOCAL CHICKEN

Ingredients:

3 pounds chicken, skinless and cut in chunks
2 onions, sliced thinly
2 garlic cloves, minced
1 can tomatoes
1 tsp salt
¼ tsp pepper
½ tsp basil
½ tsp crushed oregano
1 bay leaf
½ tsp celery seed

Cooking Directions:

Put the ingredients in order and cook for 8 hours and on low heat.

LOW FAT CHICKEN & VEGGIES

Ingredients:

8 chicken breasts, skinless and boneless
2 cans potatoes well drained
1 tsp of garlic powder
1 bottle Italian salad dressing, fat-free
1 package frozen veggies
1 can of water chestnuts
Salt and pepper

Cooking Directions:

Seasoned chicken breasts with garlic, salt and pepper.
Place the chicken at the bottom of slow cooker.
Add the rest of the ingredients.
Cook for 6 hours on high heat.
Makes 8 servings.

CHICKEN LASAGNA

Ingredients:

1 package of chicken, 9oz., cooked and diced
1 package of frozen spinach, 10oz., thawed then drained
2 cans, 11oz., cream of chicken soup
Milk, 1 can
1 carton of sour cream, 8oz.
½ cup of parmesan cheese
½ teaspoon of salt
1 onion, small and chopped
1/8 teaspoon of nutmeg
¼ teaspoon of pepper
1 cup of shredded mozzarella cheese
9 uncooked lasagne noodles

Cooking Directions:

First, prepare a huge bowl to mix in the main ingredients. Put in the chicken, then the spinach, followed by the soup and the sour cream.
Make sure this is all combined nicely by stirring it well.
Next, pour in the milk, add in the onions and continue to stir.
By now a mixture would be formed in the bowl.

Take the parmesan cheese and sprinkle it on top of the mixture, together with the salt, pepper, and nutmeg then continue to stir until it is blended in well.

Now prepare a slow cooker, you can either place in three whole lasagne noodles or split it into half if the casserole is

not big enough.
Take 1/3 of the spinach mixture and pour it on top of the noodles.
Add in 1/3 of mozzarella cheese.
Do the same process twice.
Give it an hour to cook on high, make sure the casserole is covered.
For another 5 hours, turn the fire to low.
Now the dish is ready.
Best served with toasted Italian bread and a salad of your choice.

LEMON PUCKER CHICKEN

Ingredient:

4 pieces of boneless, skinless chicken breast
1 lemon, fresh
1 teaspoon of lemon pepper
1 teaspoon of paprika

Cooking Directions:

Prepare a slow cooker and put in the chicken breasts.
Take the lemon and cut in two.
Cut one half of it into slices for putting on top of the chicken.
Use the other half to squeeze the juice on the chicken.
Next, take the paprika and lemon pepper and sprinkle on the chicken.
Put on the lid and cook on high temperature for 4 hours.
As an alternative, one tbsp of lemon juice is also good instead of using the fresh lemon.
Paprika can be replaced by garlic.
For a tasty variety, any citrus fruit can be used.

MEDITERRANEAN STYLE CHICKEN

Ingredients:

6 chicken breasts, boneless & skinless
1 can of tomato sauce (large)
1 can of tomato puree (small)
1 can of mushrooms (sliced)
1 can of ripe olives (whole or sliced)
1 tbsp of garlic
1 tbsp of lemon juice
1 tsp of oregano
1 onion (chopped)
½ c of wine or brandy (alternative)
Rice, cooked
Pinch of salt

Cooking Directions:

Make sure to rinse and clean the chicken and remove all impurities including extra fat.
Put the cleaned chicken in a slow cooker.
Separate the rice first and set it aside.
Pour the tomato sauce mixed with the puree on the chicken.
Throw in the mushrooms, olives, garlic, onion, and oregano.
Also put in the lemon juice and a dash of salt.
Now it's ready to cook.
Cover with the lid and set on low about 6-8 hours.
Best served as toppings on the rice.
Good for 6 portions.

CHICKEN STEW MEXICAN STYLE

IngredientS:

2 chicken breasts (boneless and skinless)
4 russet potatoes (medium sized)
1 can of mild salsa (15oz)
1 can of green chillies (4oz)
1 package of taco seasoning mix (1 ¼ oz)
1 can of tomato sauce (8oz)

Cooking Directions:

Clean and rinse the chicken breasts and cut into one and a half parts before putting in a slow cooker.
Skin and dice the potatoes into tiny squares and put in with the chicken.
Add the tomato sauce, salsa, chillies, and taco seasoning mix.
Cooking time is approximately 7 to 9 hours over low temperature setting.
Best served with heated soft tortillas and/or corn.

SPICED UP ROASTED CHICKEN

Ingredients:

4 teaspoons of salt
2 teaspoons of paprika
1 teaspoon of cayenne pepper
1 teaspoon of onion powder
1 teaspoon of thyme
½ teaspoon of garlic powder
½ teaspoon of pepper
1 large chicken for roasting
1 large onion

Cooking directions:

Clean both the inside and outside of the chicken carefully, removing all the internal organs. Set aside to dry.
Prepare a mixing bowl and in any order put in the spices and stir well until blended.
Make sure chicken is dry of liquid.
Varnish it over with the blended spices on the inside and out.
Once done, wrap the chicken with cellophane and place in a casserole.
Let it stay overnight in the refrigerator.
Now cut the onions into 4 parts and put it at the opening of the chicken before roasting.
Cook in a slow cooker for 9 hours at low temperature setting.
It is best to let the juice ooze from the chicken to serve as the sauce.

CHEESY CHICKEN

Ingredients:

3 whole pieces of chicken breasts (boneless)
2 cans of cream chicken soup
1 can of cheddar cheese soup

Cooking Directions:

Note: Both soups can also be self made, go to soup recipes

Clean all the excess skin and fat from the chicken. Dry with a clean cloth and embellish with salt, pepper, and garlic powder.

Place in a slow cooker and pour in the cream chicken soup followed by the cheddar cheese soup.

Cover the pan, set temperature to low and cook the whole day, at a minimum of 8 hours.

Best served as toppings for either noodles or rice.

FAST CHICKEN & NOODLES

Ingredients:

4 carrots
4 to 5 pieces of chicken
1 onion (small)
2 c of water
4 cubes of chicken bouillon
1 teaspoon of garlic salt
A dash of salt and pepper
1 pound of egg noodles

Cooking Directions:

Clean and rinse all the chicken and put inside a slow cooker.
Slice the carrots and chop the onions in small pieces and put together with the chicken.
Add the cubes, salt, pepper, and the garlic salt along with the water.
Put the setting at low temperature and cook chicken for 8 hours.
Next, take the egg noodles and boil in another pot until cooked.
Once chicken is cooked, cut it into tiny pieces.
Combine the cooked noodles and tiny pieces of chicken back into the pot.
Some cornstarch mixed evenly with water and the broth can be added to thicken the sauce.

SIMPLE CHICKEN STEW

Ingredients

1 chicken (3 pounds)
2 qts of water
1 onion
3 potatoes
2 cans of tomatoes
Lima beans (10 oz); frozen then thawed
Whole kernel corn (10 oz); frozen then partly thawed
2 tsp of salt
1 tsp of sugar (either stevia or xylitol)
¼ tsp of pepper
½ tsp of seasoned salt

Cooking Directions:

Chop the chicken and cut the onions and potatoes in small cubes then put them together with the chicken to boil. Heat in a slow cooker set on low temperature approximately 4-5 hours.
Once chicken is cooked separate the meat from the bones. Then put back only the chicken meat in the pot.
Include the beans, corn, and the cut up tomatoes.
Add in the salt, pepper, seasoned salt, and a dash of sugar (up to preference).
Continue to boil on high temperature setting for another hour.
Good for 8 portions.

EASY BARBECUE CHICKEN

Ingredients:

1 chicken
1 cup of ketchup – sugarfree (alternative, ¾ cup of xylitol sugar)
3 tbsp of Worcestershire sauce

Cooking Directions:

Clean and rinse the chicken and chop to desired portions. Make sure to get rid of all the skin.
Place the chicken in a slow cooker and add the ketchup and Worcestershire sauce.
Choose to either heat on low temperature about 8 to 10 hours or, heat on high temperature until 4 hours.

RED CHICKEN STEW

Ingredients:

Skinned chicken pieces (2.5-3 pounds)
3 c of fresh mushrooms
1 onion (large)
2 garlic cloves
¾ c of chicken broth
1 can of tomato paste (6oz)
¼ c of red wine (dry, e.g. Merlot); alternative, chicken broth
2 tbsp tapioca (quick cooking)
2 tbsp of fresh basil (snipped) or 1.5 teaspoon of crushed dried basil
¼ teaspoon of salt
¼ teaspoon of pepper
2 cups of noodles (cooked)
2 tbsp of parmesan cheese
2 teaspoons of sugar (xylitol or stevia); this is optional

Cooking Directions:

Clean and rinse the chicken and make sure to remove any extra skin.
Slice the mushrooms and onion.
Chop the garlic finely and put all these at the bottom of the slow cooker.
Position the chicken above the mushrooms, onion, and garlic in the slow cooker.
Prepare a bowl and mix in the tomato paste, broth, tapioca, chicken broth or wine, salt, pepper, dry basil (alt., fresh basil), and sugar (if preferred).
Pour in the bowl contents on the chicken and put the lid

on.
Option: Heat on low temperature setting about 7-8 hours or on high temperature setting about 3.5-4 hours.
Once chicken is done, pour the stew on top of the hot noodles and embellish with parmesan cheese.
Good for 4-6 portions.

SPECIAL BARBECUE CHICKEN

Ingredients:

4 to 6 pcs of chicken breasts (boneless)
1 bottle of barbecue sauce
½ c of vinegar (white)
½ c of xylitol sugar
1 teaspoon of mesquite seasoning
½ teaspoon of garlic powder
½ to 1 teaspoon of red pepper flakes

Cooking Directions:

Clean the chicken and put in a slow cooker.
Mix the barbecue sauce with the vinegar, sugar, garlic powder, seasoning, and red pepper flakes in a bowl.
Pour the mixture on top of the chicken and cook on low temperature setting for 5 to 6 hours.
Some recommended side dish: coleslaw, potato salad, and baked beans.

SIMPLE CHICKEN

Ingredients:

Whole chicken (3 pounds)
2 carrots
2 onions
2 stalks of celery with leaves
1 teaspoon of basil
2 teaspoons of salt
½ teaspoon of black pepper
½ cup of chicken broth (alternative, wine)

Cooking Directions:

Slice the carrots and onions and put in a slow cooker together with the celery stalks.
Clean and rinse the chicken and put on top of the vegetables.
Pour in the broth (or wine) and sprinkle with pepper, salt, and basil.
Close the lid and heat on low temperature setting from 8-10 hours or until cooked.
Alternatively, can also be cooked on high temperature setting for 3-4 hours with an additional 1 cup of water.
Take out the cooked chicken using a spatula.

CRANBERRY CHICKEN

Ingredients:

6 pcs of chicken breast (skinless, boneless)
6 pcs of green onions
½ cup of dried cranberries
½ cup of dried apples
½ teaspoon of garlic
2 tbsp of xylitol sugar or natural sweetener
2 tbsp of water
1 teaspoon of lemon juice
2 teaspoons of margarine or butter

Cooking Directions:

Clean and rinse the chicken breasts and put inside a slow cooker.
Mince the garlic and chop the onions and apples.
Combine all these with the cranberries together with the sugar and put in with the chicken.
Add in the lemon juice and water.
Brush the top of the chicken with either margarine or butter.
Put on the lid and heat on low temperature about 6 hours.
Alternatively: a seasoning of pepper and garlic salt can be used in lieu of the minced garlic

SQUASHY CHICKEN

Ingredients:

4 pieces of chicken breast (skinless, boneless)
2 carrots
2 parsnips
1 acorn squash
1 can of chicken broth (14.5 oz)
½ teaspoon of garlic salt
¼ teaspoon of pepper
¼ teaspoon of nutmeg
¼ cup of honey

Cooking Directions:

Skin and cut the carrots, parsnips, and squash.
Prepare a slow cooker and put in the carrots and parsnips first layered by the garlic salt.
Clean and rinse the chicken and position above the vegetables in the pot.
Pour the broth in the cooker; add in the squash along with the garlic salt, pepper, nutmeg, and honey.
Close the lid, set on low temperature setting and cooks for 3 hours.

SPICED APPETISER OF CHICKEN WINGS

Ingredients:

Chicken wings (4 pounds)
1 bottle of chilli sauce (12 oz)
3 tbsp of lemon juice
¼ cup of molasses
2 tbsp of Worcestershire sauce
4 drops of hot pepper sauce
1 tbsp of hot salsa
2 teaspoons of chilli powder
1 teaspoon of garlic powder
2 teaspoons of salt

Cooking Directions:

This recipe is recommended for any type of gatherings.
Place the chicken wings in a slow cooker.
Get a bowl and mix in the chilli sauce, hot pepper sauce, Worcestershire sauce, salsa, molasses, and lemon juice.
Add in the salt, chilli powder, and garlic powder.
Pour over the mixture on the chicken wings.
Close the lid and put setting on low temperature to cook for 4 hours.

CHICKPEA CHICK CASSEROLE

Ingredients:

2 whole chicken breasts (deboned and skinned)
Celery heart
1 onion (medium)
2 cans of chopped tomatoes
Medium salsa or picante sauce (16oz)
1 can of chick peas (alternative, 1 package of white kidney beans)
Mushrooms (6oz)
Coconut or olive oil

Cooking Directions:

Clean and cut the chicken breasts in half size pieces and fry in a pan with 1 tbsp of oil until golden.
Cut up the onion, celery, and mushrooms.
Combine with the tomatoes and chick peas (or white kidney beans) and put together in the chicken in a slow cooker and let it broil about 6 to 8 hours in low temperature setting.
For spice lovers, include the hot salsa or picante sauce.
Can be eaten either with taco chips or bread.

EVERYDAY CHICKEN STEW

Ingredients:

2 pounds of chicken breasts (boneless, skinless)
2 cups of chicken broth (fat free)
3 cups of potatoes
1 cup of onion
1 cup of celery
1 cup of carrots
1 teaspoon of paprika
½ teaspoon of pepper
½ teaspoon of rubbed sage
½ teaspoon of dried thyme
Tomato paste (6oz, no salt)
¼ cup of cold water
3 tbsp of cornstarch

Cooking Directions:

Clean and cut the chicken breasts into 1 inch cubes and place in a slow cooker. Slice the carrots and the celery.
Make sure carrots are cut into thin parts.
Take out the potato skin and cut into squares.
Chop the onion and combine all these into the cooker.
Include the broth, tomato paste and sprinkle the pepper and paprika. Put in the rubbed sage and dried thyme.
Close the lid and cook on high temperature about 4 hours.
Get a bowl and mix the cornstarch and water.
Blend to an even mixture. Pour this on the chicken.
Close the lid and cook for another 30 minutes or just before the vegetables turn soft.

Slow Cooker Beans

BARBECUE BEAN SOUP

Ingredients:

Great northern beans (1 pound, soaked)
2 teaspoons of salt
1 onion (medium)
1/8 teaspoon of ground pepper
6 c of water
¾ c of barbecue sauce

Cooking Directions:

Chop the onions and combine it with the beans in a slow cooker.
Add in the salt, ground pepper, and water.
Close the lid and cook in low temperature for 10-16 hours.
Mix in the barbecue sauce ahead of serving.

BLACK BEAN SOUP

Ingredients:

2 pcs of onions
2 garlic cloves
3 tbsp of butter
1 lb of black beans (immersed for one night)
1 celery stalk
1 pc of bay leaf
½ c of dry white wine (sherry)
Salt
Pepper

Cooking Directions:

Mince the garlic and cut the onions. Use the butter to sauté the garlic and onion until golden brown.
Strain the black beans. Chop the celery and put in a slow cooker. Pour in the water and add the beans and bay leaf.
Set to boil on high temperature about 2 hours.
Reduce temperature to low and continue another 8-10 hours more.
After boiling, take out the bay leaf and mash the ingredients of the soup.
Next, pour in the sherry and stir.
Add a bit of pepper and salt. Continue to cook for a few minutes.
Prepare servings embellished with slices of lemon, diced parsley, and hard boiled eggs.

WHITE BEAN SOUP

Ingredients:

1 pound of white beans (small)
8 cups of water
1 cup of onion
1 cup of parsley
1 cup of celery
1 teaspoon of salt
¼ teaspoon of pepper
1 piece of bay leaf

Cooking Directions:

Chop the celery and parsley into fine pieces.
Likewise, cut the onions into small squares.
Prepare a slow cooker and put in the chopped celery, parsley, and onions together with the beans.
Add the water then put in the bay leaf.
Sprinkle salt and pepper.
Close the lid and set to cook for 8 to 10 hours at low temperature or up till beans turn soft.

BLACK BEAN CHILI STEW

Ingredients:

1 pkt of black beans (dry)
2 tbsp of oil
6 cloves of garlic
2 pcs of onions
¼ teaspoon of red pepper flakes (amount varies on spice level preferred)
1 tbsp of chilli powder
1 tbsp of cumin, grinded
1 teaspoon of oregano (dried)
1 pc of bay leaf
1 can of crushed tomatoes (28oz, juice)
2 cups of water
1 can of tomato paste (6 oz)
1 tbsp of wine vinegar (red)
2 cans of variety beans (own choice)

Cooking Directions:

Boil the variety of beans in a large amount of water overnight under low temperature.
Drain the water and rinse the beans the next day and allow to dry.
Chop the onions; crush the garlic and red pepper flakes then sauté all three together for a minute.
Next, include the cumin and chilli powder, continue sauté for 2 minutes.
Get a slow cooker and pour in the sautéed mixture.
Add the black beans, tomatoes & tomato paste, bay leaf,

red wine vinegar, and water.
Mix the ingredients well and boil in low temperature the whole day.
Just add the variety of beans 1-1.5 hours earlier, prior to serving.
To enhance the flavour, prepare some cheese to grate, mince some onions & parsley, and sour cream. Top up with the prepared extra embellishments.

VARIOUS MIXED BEAN SOUP

Ingredients:

16 oz of various beans (alternative, 1 pkg of 16 Bean Soup Mix)
3 pcs of bay leaf
1 tbsp of oregano
2 cans of chicken stock (fat free); (alternative flavour, 2 cans of tomatoes with water)
3 celery stalks (optional)
3 pcs of carrots
1 onion (large)
3 garlic cloves

Cooking Directions:

Note: any preferred stock of choice can be used for this soup
Clean and rinse the beans thoroughly and put inside a slow cooker.
Pour in the stock (or tomatoes) then the bay leaves and oregano.
Add in an adequate amount of water that would overlay the mixture at least one to two inches.
Boil in high temperature about 2 hours.
While waiting to boil, get the carrots diced, the celery chopped (which is an optional ingredient), the onion cut, and the garlic sliced.
Additional ingredients like zucchini, chopped cabbage, and diced red potatoes can also be added for more variety.
Once boiled, throw in the cut vegetables and spices.

Change temperature to low and continue cooking for 3 hours.

For a spicy version, some mashed red pepper or cayenne can be added.

Serving suggestions: toppings on rice, bread of choice, or served alone.

SIMPLE BLACK BEAN DISH

Ingredients:

1 pound of black beans (dried) or turtle beans
Jar of your preferred salsa (16 oz)

Cooking Directions:

Clean and rinse the beans carefully, making sure to remove all unnecessary impurities.
Immerse in adequate amount of water and leave overnight.
The following day, strain the beans and put in a slow cooker.
Add the salsa of your choice and pour in a sufficient amount of water to cover the beans.
Close the lid, set to low temperature, and cook for 8 to 10 hours.

CHICK AND BAKED BEANS

2 cans of kidney beans (white)
2 cans of kidney beans (red)
2 cans of black beans
1 can of chick peas
2 onions
2 tbsp of moist mustard
1 cup of molasses
½ cup of brown sugar
¾ cup of maple syrup
Clean, rinse, and strain all the beans.

Cooking Directions:

Cut up the onions and put in first in the slow cooker.
Then add all the beans and chick peas.
Sprinkle the brown sugar and pour the maple syrup and molasses.
Next, add the mustard.
Leave it as it is and cook over high temperature approximately 6 hours while mixing one time after heating for 4-4.5 hours.
Can be served with toasted bread or pasta of choice.

CHILI BEAN SOUP

Ingredients:

2 cans of black beans (15 oz)
2 cans of green chiles (4.5 oz)
1 can of Mexican Stewed tomatoes (14.5 oz)
1 can of tomatoes, diced (14.5 oz)
1 can of whole kernel corn (11 oz)
4 pcs of green onions
2-3 tbsp of chilli powder
½ teaspoon of dried garlic
1 teaspoon of cumin, grounded (optional)

Cooking Directions:

Rinse and drain the black beans and whole kernel corn.
Chop up the chiles, green onions, and garlic.
Get a 3-5 quarts slow cooker and place the black beans, whole kernel corn, chiles, onions, and garlic inside.
Pour in the tomatoes with all their juices.
Add in the chilli powder and (optional) cumin.
Close the lid and choose to cook it either on low temperature the whole day or high temperature for 5-6 hours.
Approximately serves 8 portions.
Suggestions for serving: top up with cheddar cheese cut into slivers and some lite sour cream.

BLACK EYED PEA STEW

Ingredients:

1 bag of black eyed peas (16oz, dried)
1 can of tomatoes with jalapenos (14.5oz, diced)
1 can of tomatoes with mild green chiles (14.5oz, diced)
2 cans chicken broth (10.5oz each)
1 celery stalk
Salt
Pepper

Cooking Directions:

Follow the procedure on how to soak the black eyed peas found at the bag.
This must be done prior to cooking.
Get a slow cooker and pour in the tomatoes.
Chop the celery and add in together with the broth.
Put a bit of pepper and salt.
Then add the peas.
Heat at low temperature about 8 to 10 hours.
Dish out on rice, pasta, or noodle.

Slow Cooker Beef

BARBECUE STEAK CASSEROLE

Ingredients:

1.5 pound, 1.5 thick chuck steak (boneless)
1 garlic clove
¼ c of wine vinegar
1 tbsp of brown sugar
1 teaspoon of paprika
2 tbsp of Worcestershire sauce
½ c of organic tomato sauce (no sugar)
1 teaspoon of salt
1 teaspoon of mustard (dry)
¼ teaspoon of black pepper

Cooking Directions:

Slice the beef in a slanted way about an inch wide. Put all the slices in a slow cooker.
Take the garlic and crush it.
Get a bowl and pour the tomato sauce.
Add the Worcestershire sauce, wine vinegar, and garlic.
Put in the mustard, brown sugar, salt, pepper, and paprika.
Mix all thoroughly.
Pour the mixture on the beef and close the lid.
Set temperature to low and cook approximately 3-5 hours.

BARBECUE BEEF STEW

Ingredients:

2 pounds of stewing meat
3 tbsp of oil
1 cup of onion
½ cup of green pepper
1 garlic clove (large)
½ teaspoon of salt
1/8 teaspoon of pepper
2 cups of beef stock
1 can of tomatoes (8oz)
1 can of mushrooms (4oz)
1/3 cup of barbecue sauce
3 tbsp of cornstarch
¼ cup of cold water

Cooking Directions:

Prepare a slow cooker and put in the meat after cleaning.
Slice up the onion, green pepper, garlic and sauté this using the oil.
Next, add in the tomatoes, beef stock, barbecue sauce, and mushrooms.
Then sprinkle in the salt and pepper.
Combine this cooked mixture with the meat in the slow cooker. Heat up on low temperature setting approximately 8 to 10 hours. When the meat is almost done, prepare a bowl and mix the cornstarch and water thoroughly.
Pour this over the stew to make the sauce thicker.
Best served as toppings on rice.

CHILI MINCE DINNER

Ingredients:

2 pounds of ground beef
1 onion (large)
1 green pepper (large)
1 jalapeno pepper (large)
Chilli powder
Garlic salt
Salt
Pepper
Sugar (stevia or xylitol)
2 cans of tomatoes (crushed)
1 can of tomato puree
1 can of kidney beans
2 cans of chilli hot beans

Cooking Directions:

Cut up the green pepper, onion and sauté together.
Add in the beef and continue until cooked.
Put in the sliced up jalapeno pepper and a dash of salt and pepper. Sprinkle a bit of chilli powder, garlic salt, and sugar to spruce up the taste.
Leave it to cool for an hour.
Get a slow cooker and place the cooked beef in.
Add the beans, tomatoes, and tomato puree.
Heat in the cooker the whole day.
Serving suggestion: prepare a day before and let cool in the refrigerator overnight. Serve warm on the following day.

ALL DAY BEEF STEW

Ingredients;

2 to 3 pounds of cubed beef (boneless)
½ cup of flour
¼ cup of margarine or butter
1 onion
1 teaspoon of salt
1 teaspoon of pepper
1 garlic clove
2 cups of beef stock
1 pc of bay leaf
1 teaspoon of paprika
Optional: 1 teaspoon of Worcestershire sauce
Baby carrots
Baby potatoes

Cooking Directions:

Roll the beef cubes on the flour and fry in butter on a pan till cooked.
Remove the extra fat after frying and place the beef in a slow cooker.
Slice up the onion, crush the garlic and sprinkle over the beef.
Add the butter, salt, pepper, paprika, bay leaf, and pour in the stock.
If vegetables are preferred, some baby carrots and baby potatoes would be a nice combination.
For a tangy taste, add the Worcestershire sauce.
Once ready, set cooker temperature to low about 7 to 10 hours. Change setting to high if beef becomes tender.

For a thicker sauce, add more flour and a bit of water into the pot and continue to heat another 30 to 40 minutes. Can be dished out with either rice or salad.

LATE BREAKFAST BRUNCH CASSEROLE

Ingredients:

1.5 pound ground beef
1 onion (large)
2 tbsp of olive oil (alternative, butter)
2 cloves of garlic
Mushrooms
2 teaspoons of salt
½ teaspoon of nutmeg
½ teaspoon of oregano leaf
½ pack of spinach (thawed, strained)
3 tbsp of flour
6 eggs
¼ cup of milk
½ cup of cheddar cheese

Cooking Directions:

Slice the mushrooms and chop the onions nicely.
Sauté this together with the ground beef in olive oil until slightly cooked and then drain the oil.
Prepare a slow cooker covered with oil and put in the beef.
Drain and chop the spinach and add to the beef.
Crush the garlic and add this too.
Next, put in the flour, salt, nutmeg, and oregano leaf.
Mix well to an even texture.
In a bowl, combine the beaten eggs and heated milk and blend together.
Pour this with the beef in the cooker.
Sprinkle some more nutmeg and put on the lid.

Set to low temperature about 7-10 hours until beef solidifies.
Grate the cheese and sprinkle on top prior to serving.
Good for 6-8 portions.

BEEFY BEAN LUNCH

Ingredients

1.5 pounds stew beef
1 tbsp of prepared mustard
1 tbsp of taco seasoning
½ teaspoon of salt
¼ teaspoon of pepper
2 cloves of garlic
1 can of diced tomatoes (16oz, undrained)
1 onion (medium)
1 can of kidney beans
1 can of chilli beans
1 can black beans

Cooking Directions:

Mix in a big bowl the taco seasoning, mustard, pepper, salt and garlic.
Add in the ground beef and continue mixing thoroughly.
Place the mixture in a slow cooker.
Add the beans, tomatoes, and the chopped onion.
Close the lid and heat at low temperature about 6 to 8 hours.
Good to serve as rice toppings.

FOUR BEAN CHILI

Ingredients:

1 to 2 lbs ground beef
2 cans of chilli hot beans
2 cans of kidney beans (dark red)
2 cans of kidney beans
2 cans of pinto beans
2 cans of rotel tomatoes
1 pkg of chilli seasoning

Cooking Directions:

Drain all the pinto and kidney beans of its liquid.
Sauté the ground beef until brown.
Get a slow cooker and transfer the beef, chilli hot beans, drained beans, tomatoes, and seasoning.
Set to cook for 10 hours at low temperature.
Good to serve along with pasta, rice, bread, couscous or quinoa.

BEEF BOURGUIGNON

Ingredients:

1 c of red wine (dry)
2 tbsp of olive oil
1 onion (large, sliced)
½ teaspoon of thyme
2 tbsp of parsley (chopped)
1 pc of bay leaf
¼ tsp of pepper
2 lbs of 1.5 inch squares stew beef
12 white onions (small)
½ lb of mushrooms
2 garlic cloves
1 teaspoon of salt

Cooking Directions:

Prepare the beef to be marinated one night in the fridge or about 3 hours. Put the beef in a container and add in the red wine, olive oil, onion, thyme, parsley, pepper, and the bay leaf. Mix evenly.
After marinating, separate the beef and cook in a pan. Transfer the cooked beef in a slow cooker and add in the onions, mushrooms, garlic and salt.
Use the marinade generously over the beef.
Set to low and cook for 8 to 10 hours.

LUXURY BLACK BEAN CHILI

Ingredients:

¾ c of black beans (cooked)
1 pound cubed stew beef
3 tbsp of oil
¼ c of onion (chopped)
¼ c of green peppers (chopped)
½ c of green chillies (diced)
3 tbsp of tomato paste
3-4 cubes of beef bouillon (alternative, beef base)
¼ teaspoon of ground cumin
1 teaspoon of garlic (minced)
½ teaspoon of salt
½ teaspoon pepper
1 c of cheddar cheese (shredded); (alternative, Monterrey Jack)

Cooking Directions:

Sauté the beef with the green pepper and onion using the oil.
Transfer to a slow cooker and add in the black beans, green chillies, tomato paste, beef cubes, cumin, salt, garlic, and pepper.
Set to low and heat for 6-8 hours.
Garnish each serving with the shredded cheese.

BEEF BURGUNDY

Ingredients:

2 lbs of 1 in cubes sirloin tip (alternative, round steak)
¼ c of flour
1 tsp of salt
½ tsp of seasoned salt
¼ tsp of marjoram
¼ tsp of thyme
¼ tsp of pepper
1 garlic clove (minced)
1 beef bouillon cube (crushed)
1 c of burgundy wine
2 tbsp of cornstarch (mix in water)
Optional: fresh mushrooms

Cooking Directions:

Prepare a greased pan using butter.
Cover steak with the flour and fry making sure to flip it to get an even cooking.
 Once done, put in a slow cooker and add the wine, beef cubes, garlic, pepper, thyme, marjoram, salt, and seasoned salt.
Close the lid, set to cook at low temperature until steak turns soft (6-8hours).
Add in the cornstarch and mushrooms (optional) then switch to cook at high temperature for 15 minutes.
Makes about 6 portions.

BEEF BURGER STROGANOFF

Ingredients:

1.5 pounds of ground beef (lean)
1 onion (small, chopped)
2 tablespoons of flour
¼ teaspoon of paprika
1 teaspoon of salt
1 can of cream of mushroom soup (10 3/4oz, condensed)
2 tbsp of red wine (dry)
1 c of dairy sour cream
6-8 hamburger buns (buttered, toasted)

Cooking Directions:

Sauté the ground beef until finely cooked. Remove the excess oil and transfer to a slow cooker. Add in the flour, onion, salt, and paprika. Pour the cream soup and wine while slowly stirring. Close the lid and set to cook at low temperature for 4-5 hours. Once done, mix the sour cream in the pot.
Prepare the buns and ladle mixture on top. For a creamy taste, use buttered noodles instead of buns. Good for 6-8 portions.

SPICY PEPPER BEEF FAJITAS

Ingredients:

1.5 pounds of beef flank steak
1 c of onion (chopped)
1 green sweet pepper (cut to ½ in pcs)
1 jalapeno pepper (chopped)
1 tbsp of cilantro
2 cloves of garlic (minced); (alternative, ¼ tsp of garlic powder)
1 teaspoon of chilli powder
1 teaspoon of cumin (ground)
1 teaspoon of coriander (ground)
½ teaspoon of salt
1 can of tomatoes (8oz, chopped)
Flour tortillas (12x8in)

Cooking Directions:

Slice the steak into 6 parts and place in a slow cooker. Add in the jalapeno pepper, green pepper, onion, garlic, cilantro, cumin, chilli powder, salt, coriander, and lastly the tomatoes. Close the lid and set to cook either at low temperature 8 to 10 hours or high temperature 4 to 5 hours.
Once cooked, cut the meat into tiny pieces and stir the mixture. Prepare the tortillas and ladle mixture on it topped by your favourite garnish. Then it's ready to be rolled.
Suggested garnishes: grated cheddar cheese, salsa, guacamole, sour cream

SPICED VEGETABLE & BEEF SOUP

Ingredients:

3 onions (medium, sliced)
1 pound of ½ in carrot slices
4 parsnips (cut to ½ in slices)
2 pcs of bay leaf
4 garlic cloves (minced)
1 tbsp of fresh thyme (crushed); (alternative, 1 teaspoon of dried thyme)
½ teaspoon of pepper
2 tbsp of tapioca (quick cooking)
1.5 pounds of 1in cubed beef stew meat
1 can of beef broth (14.5oz)
1 can of beer (12oz)

Cooking Directions:

Get ready a 5-6 qt slow cooker and put in the onions, carrot slices, parsnips, bay leaves, garlic, dried thyme, and pepper. Take the meat and place above this. Throw in the tapioca then pour the beer and beef broth. Cover and choose to either cook at low temperature about 10-12 hours or at high temperature about 5-6 hours. Once done, take out the bay leaves and sprinkle fresh thyme (optional) prior to serving.

CARROT, POTATO & BEEF POT ROAST

Ingredients:

1.5 to 2 pounds of meat for pot roast
2 tbsp of olive oil
Salt
Pepper
Mixed dried herbs
2 pcs of onion
4 garlic cloves
½ c of red wine (or volume as preferred)
1 pc of bay leaf
Baby carrots
Potatoes
Note: Quantity of potatoes and carrots can be adjusted to suit desired portions

Cooking Directions:

Prepare a slow cooker and put in the sliced onions and skinned garlic, followed by the potatoes and carrots. Take the meat and smear it with olive oil, salt, pepper, and herbs. Add on top of the cooker. Next pour in the red wine and add the bay leaf. Set to cook at low temperature for 8 to 10 hours. Flip the meat every now and then.

CLASSIC BEEF & POTATO STEW

Ingredients:

1 pound of beef bourguignon (low cost cut can be used)
3 sweet potatoes (large, slice to 1in)
2 cans of beef bouillon (alternative, broth or consommé)
2 cans of tomato paste (small, organic)
3 to 4 small quantities of mixed vegetables (e.g., frozen green peas and carrots)
1 pound of fresh mushrooms (cut to 4 pcs)
1 onion (large, diced)
2 garlic cloves (minced)
¼ c of flour

Cooking Directions:

Boil the sweet potatoes until soft and set aside. Slice the meat into small pieces and coat with the flour. Sauté meat with garlic and oil until browned. Prepare a slow cooker and mix together the tomato paste and beef bouillon. Add in the potatoes, vegetables of choice, and onions. Pour in sufficient water and set to cook at low temperature maximum of 5 hours. The mushrooms and other frozen vegetables can be added once nearly done. If thicker stew is preferred, flour mixed with some water can also be included.

QUICK-PREP BEEF STEW

Ingredients:

1 pkg of stew beef
Cream of potato soup (1 can)
Cream of mushroom soup (1 can)

Cooking Directions:

Place all the ingredients in a slow cooker and stir in with 1 to 1.5 cans of water. Set to cook at high temperature for 7 to 8 hours. Good to serve as toppings on various types of cooked rice.

MUSHROOM BEEF STROGANOFF

Ingredients:

2 pounds of top round steak
1 pound of fresh mushrooms
1 onion (medium)
¼ teaspoon of thyme
¾ c of dry sherry (alternative, dry white wine); amount can vary depending on taste
¾ c of beef broth
¾ teaspoon of tomato paste (alternative taste, dry mustard)
¼ teaspoon of garlic salt
1 ½ c of sour cream
½ c of flour

Cooking Directions:

Cut the steak into thin slices across the grain and put inside a slow cooker. Cut up the onions and mushrooms and throw into the pot. Add the thyme, dry sherry, broth, tomato paste (or mustard), sprinkle the garlic salt and mix together well.
Set to cook at low temperature about 8 hours. After, stir in the sour cream and flour and turn to high temperature another 40 minutes. Good as toppings on noodles or rice.

SPEEDY-PREP BEEF STROGANOFF

Ingredients:

Cream of mushroom soup (1 can)
Onion soup mix (1 pkg)
Mushroom (1 pkg)
Beef stew meat (1 pkg)
Sour cream
1 onion
Salt
Pepper
Cooked egg noodles

Ingredients:

Ready a slow cooker and place the meat inside. Cut the onion into rings and toss into the meat. Add the onion soup mix, mushrooms, and pour in the cream of mushroom soup. Set to cook at low temperature the whole day. Once done, add the sour cream prior to serving. Good as toppings for egg noodles.

MEXICAN BEAN & BEEF SOUP

Ingredients:

2 pounds of rump roast
1 pack of taco seasoning
1 can of Mexican style tomatoes (15oz, diced)
1 can of green chiles (small)
1 can of tomato sauce (8oz)
1 onion
2 cubes of beef bouillon
2 cans of kidney beans (15oz, red)
Cheddar cheese

Cooking Directions:

Slice the roast to small cubes and coat with taco seasoning. Prepare a slow cooker and add in the tomato sauce, tomatoes, green chiles, onion, and beef cubes together with the coated roast.
Close the lid and heat at low temperature until roast turns soft (approximately 6 hours).
Rinse and drain the beans. Add to the pot and continue to cook for 30 minutes.
Add grated cheese on top prior to serving as well as any preferred garnishes.

CLASSIC BLACK BEAN CHILI

Ingredients:

¾ c of black beans (cooked)
1 pound of stew beef (cut into cubes)
3 tbsp of oil
¼ c of onion (chopped)
¼ c of green peppers (chopped)
½ c of green chiles (diced)
3 tbsp of tomato paste
3-4 cubes of beef bouillon (alternative, beef base)
¼ teaspoon of cumin (ground)
1 teaspoon of garlic (minced)
½ teaspoon of salt
½ teaspoon of pepper
1 c of cheddar cheese (alternative, Monterrey Jack)

Cooking Directions:

Cook the beef with the green peppers and onions using the oil. Prepare a slow cooker and put in the black beans, green chiles, tomato paste, and beef cubes. Add the cooked beef and put in the rest of the seasonings. Set to cook at low temperature for 6-8 hours. Grate the cheese and sprinkle on top of each serving.

SPICED BEEF & CABBAGE CASSEROLE

Ingredients:

2 lb. ground beef
1 head cabbage, shredded
1 small onion, chopped
1 (16ounce) can tomatoes
broth or tomato juice to cover bottom of pot
Garlic salt, thyme, red pepper and a bit of oregano

Directions:

Brown ground beef and drain. Shred cabbage and chop onion. Put in broth or other liquid to cover bottom of pot. Layer cabbage, onion, spices, meat, and garlic salt. Repeat layers ending with beef.
Top with tomatoes, undrained and a dusting of oregano. Cook on high for 1 hour. Stir all together.
Cook on low heat until ready to eat, 8-10 hours. Makes 3-4 servings.

ONION & GARLIC BEEF CHILI

Ingredients:

2 onions, chopped
2 cloves garlic (I use the minced kind that comes in a jar)
1 lb. lean hamburger
2 tablespoon chili powder
cumin to taste (I leave this out)
2 cans (16 ounce ea.) tomatoes
2 cans tomato soup
2 cans kidney beans, drained
salt and pepper to taste
optional: shredded cheese or sour cream for topping

Directions:

Cook onions and garlic in 2 tablespoon oil until the onions are yellow. Add hamburger and cook till browned. Stir in chili powder and optional cumin; cook 2 minutes more. Meanwhile, in slow cooker, combine remaining ingredients. Stir in browned meat mixture. Cover and cook on Low setting for 8-10 hours. To serve: ladle chili into bowls. Top with optional shredded cheese or sour cream, if desired.

SEASONED CARNE GISADA

Ingredients:

3 lbs beef stew meat
2 cans diced tomatoes with green chilies or make your own
from fresh
salt and pepper to taste
3 cloves garlic minced
1 cup chopped onion
3 tablespoon flour
½ tsp cumin
½tsp oregano
1 tsp chili powder
¼ cup water, 1 diced bell pepper

Directions:

Place stew meat, ¼ cup water, salt and pepper in slow cooker. Turn heat to high and let simmer for 1 ½ hours. Drain juice from tomatoes into measuring cup. Add tomatoes garlic and onions to slow cooker STIR let simmer on high for 30 minutes. Add cumin, oregano, and chili powder and stir. Blend juice and enough water to equal 1½ cups liquid and flour stir into mixture. Let cook on LOW for 3-4 hours until sauce is nice and thick. Serve with warm flour tortillas.

SPEEDY-PREP BEEF CHILI

Ingredients:

1 lb ground beef, cooked and rinsed
60-70 ounces rinsed light or dark kidney beans
16 ounces tomato paste
16 ounces peeled chopped tomatoes (reserve liquid)
½ small onion, chopped
1 small green pepper, chopped
1 package chili seasonings
cayenne pepper to taste, if desired

Directions:

Put all ingredients in the slow cooker and cook on low until you are ready, I'd recommend at least 5 hours so the peppers and onions are cooked soft. Use the reserved tomato liquid if it seems too thick for your taste. We serve with tortillas, cheese, sour cream, and salsa!

GREEK-STYLE ONION BEEF STEW

Ingredients:

3 pounds of stewing beef
1 ½ pounds small onions (about 7)
3 cloves garlic, minced
28 ounce can tomatoes
½ cup beef stock
5 ½ ounce can tomato paste
2 tablespoon red wine vinegar
2 tsp dried oregano & ½ tsp each salt & pepper
½ cup all purpose flour
½ cup cold water
1 sweet green pepper, chopped
Decoration: ½ c. feta cheese, 2 tablespoon. chopped fresh parsley

Directions:

Cut beef into 1 inch cubes, trimming off any fat. Cut onions into wedges. Put meat & onions into slow cooker along with garlic & tomatoes. Combine beef stock, vinegar, oregano, salt & pepper and add to slow cooker, stirring gently to blend. Cook on Low for 8-9 hours or High for 6 hours. Add flour & water mixture and chopped green pepper. Cook on high for 15 minutes or until thickened. Serve sprinkled with feta & parsley.

CLASSIC CHILI CON CARNE

Ingredients:

4 pounds ground beef
3 tablespoons shortening
2 cups chopped onion
2 garlic cloves -- crushed
4 tablespoons chili powder
3 beef bouillon cubes -- crushed
1 ½ teaspoons paprika
1 teaspoon oregano
1 teaspoon ground cumin
½ teaspoon cayenne pepper
½ cup beef stock
1 can tomatoes - 28 ounce.
1 can tomato paste - 8 ounce
4 cans red kidney beans - 1 lb cans

Directions:

Heat shortening in skillet and brown beef, discard fat. Combine all ingredients in removable liner, stirring well. Place liner in base. Cover and cook on low 8-10 hours; high 4-5 hours or auto 6-7 hours.

MEXICAN-STYLE BEEF & BEAN CHILI

Ingredients:

2 (15½ ounce) cans red kidney beans, drained
1 (28 ounce) can tomatoes, cut up
1 c. chopped celery
1 c. chopped onion
1 (6 ounce) can tomato paste
½ c. chopped green pepper
1 (4 ounce) can green chili peppers, drained and chopped
2 tablespoon. sugar
1 bay leaf
½ tsp. garlic powder
1 tsp. salt
1 tsp. dried, crushed marjoram
Dash of pepper
1 lb. ground beef

Directions:

In skillet brown ground beef and drain. In slow cooker combine all ingredients. Cover, cook on low heat for 8 to 10 hours. Remove bay leaf and stir before serving. Approximately 10 servings

Slow Cooker Vegetables

CREAMY ASPARAGUS & CHEESE CASSEROLE

Ingredients:
2 cans sliced asparagus, (10 ounce each)
1 can cream of celery soup, (10 ounce)
2 hard cooked eggs, thinly sliced
1 cup grated cheddar cheese
½ cup coarsely crushed saltines or Ritz crackers
1 teaspoon butter

Directions:

Place drained asparagus in lightly buttered slow cooker. Combine soup and cheese. Top asparagus with sliced eggs, soup mixture, then the cracker crumbs. Dot with butter. Cover and cook on low for 4 to 6 hours.

CHEESY SCALLOPED POTATOES

Ingredients:

7 to 9 medium potatoes, thinly sliced
1 cup cold water
½ tsp cream of tartar
3 tablespoon butter
1 medium onion, thinly sliced
¼ cup all-purpose flour
1 teaspoon salt & ¼ teaspoon ground black pepper
1 can (10 x ¾ ounces) condensed cream of mushroom soup
4 ounce American cheese, slices or shredded

Directions:

Toss potato slices in 1 cup water and ½ teaspoon cream of tartar, then drain. Put half of sliced potatoes in a buttered or greased 3 ½ to 4-quart slow cooker. Top with half of onion slices, half of the flour, half of the salt and half of the pepper. Dot with half of the butter. Repeat layers; dot with remaining butter. Spoon soup over the top.
Cover and cook on low 7 to 9 hours, or high 3 to 4 hrs. Add cheese about 30 minutes before serving.
Double ingredients for a 5-6-quart slow cooker.

QUICK-PREP CHEESE & BROCCOLI SOUP

Ingredients:

2 c. cooked noodles
1 (10 ounce) pkg. frozen chopped broccoli, thawed
3 tablespoon. chopped onions
2 tablespoon. butter
1 tablespoon. flour
2 cups shredded American cheese
Salt to taste
5 ½ c. milk

Directions:

Combine all ingredients in slow cooker. Stir well. Cook on low for 4 hours. Makes 8 servings.

SLOW-COOKED ARTICHOKE DISH

Ingredients:

5 artichokes, remove stalks and tough leaves
1 ½ ts salt
8 peppercorns
2 stalks celery, cut up
½ lemon, sliced
2 c. boiling water

Directions:

Combine all ingredients in slow cooker. Cook on high 4 - 5 hours.

ONION & POTATO GREEN BEAN CASSEROLE

Ingredients:

About 6 cups fresh trimmed and cut green beans (about 2 pounds) or 2 x 16-ounce packages frozen cut green beans
4 to 6 medium red-skinned potatoes, sliced about 1/4-inch
1 large onion, sliced
1 tsp dried dill weed
1 tsp salt
½ teaspoon pepper

Directions:

1 can cream of chicken soup or other cream soup, undiluted, or use about 1 cup of homemade seasoned white sauce, velouté or cheese sauce margarine.

Lightly grease slow cooker with butter. Layer sliced potatoes, sliced onion and green beans, sprinkling with dill and salt and pepper as you go. Dot with margarine, about 1 tablespoon total, and add about 2 tablespoons of water. Cover and cook on high for 4 hours (low, about 8 hours). Stir in soup or sauce; turn to low and cook an additional 30 minutes or leave on warm until serving time or up to 4 hours. Serves 6 to 8.

QUICK-PREP SEASONED CAPONATA

Ingredients:

1 lb plum tomatoes chopped
1 eggplant in 1/2" pieces
2 med zucchini in 1/2" pieces
1 onion finely chopped
3 stalks celery sliced
½ c. chopped parsley
2 tablespoon red wine vinegar
1 tablespoon brown sugar (or natural alternatives)
¼ c. raisins
¼ c. tomato paste
1 tsp salt
¼ tsp freshly ground black pepper
3 tablespoon oil cured black olives (optional)
2 tablespoon capers (optional)

Directions:

Combine tomatoes, eggplant, zucchini, celery, onion, parsley, vinegar, sugar, raisins, tomato paste, salt & pepper in slow cooker. Cook, covered on low heat for 5 ½ hours. Do not remove cover during cooking. Stir in olives & capers, if using. Serve warm or cold.

SLOW COOKER RED CABBAGE

Ingredients:

1 large head of red cabbage, washed and coarsely sliced
2 med onions coarsely chopped
6 tart apples, cored & quartered
2 tsp. salt
2 c. hot water
3 tablespoon sugar (natural alternative xylitol or stevia)
2/3 cup cider vinegar
6 tablespoon butter

Directions:

Place all ingredients in the slow cooker in order listed. Cover and cook on low 8 to 10 hours (High: 3 hours). Stir well before serving.

CHEESY POTATO CASSEROLE

Ingredients:

2 lb. pkg. frozen hash brown potatoes (partially thawed)
2 x 10 ounce cans cheddar cheese soup
1 x 13 ounce can evaporated milk
1 can French fried onion rings, divided
Salt and pepper to taste

Directions:

Combine potatoes, soup, milk, and half the can of onion rings; Pour into greased slow cooker and add salt and pepper. Cover and cook on low for 8 to 9 hours or high for 4 hours. Sprinkle the rest of the onion rings of top before serving.

SLOW-COOKED CREAMY ARTICHOKE & CHEESE DIP

Ingredients:

8 ounces process American cheese (Velveeta)
1 can (10ounce) 98% fat-free cream of mushroom soup
2 tsp Worcestershire sauce
¼ cup evaporated milk
1 teaspoon dry mustard
1½ c. shredded cheddar cheese
1/3 c. chopped roasted red pepper
1 can artichoke hearts, drained and coarsely chopped

Directions:

Combine all ingredients in the slow cooker. Cover and cook on low for 2 to 3 hours, until melted.
Stir well and serve with assorted crackers, bread cubes, or chips. You can also use this dip with cooked pasta for a delicious macaroni and cheese!

CAULIFLOWER, CHEESE & BROCCOLI DINNER

Ingredients:

1 (10 ounce) pkg frozen cauliflower, thawed
1 (10 ounce) pkg frozen broccoli, thawed
1 can Cheddar cheese soup
salt and pepper to taste
¼ cup shredded cheddar cheese, if desired

Directions:

Place broccoli and cauliflower in crockery pot. Top with soup. Season with salt and pepper. Cover and cook on low for 4 to 5 hours. About 20 minutes before done, top with cheddar cheese if used. Serves 6 to 8.

CHEESY BROCCOLI SOUP

Ingredients:

4 c. water
4 chicken bouillon cubes or veg cubes
¼ c. chopped onion
2 c. diced potatoes
1 bag frozen, chopped broccoli
2 cans cream of chicken soup
½ -1 lb. Velveeta cheese, cubed

Directions:

Mix water, bouillon cubes, onions, potatoes and broccoli in a slow cooker. Cook on high until broccoli is thawed. Add cream of chicken soup and cheese, to taste, to mixture. Turn slow cooker on low and cook for 2 hours.

CLASSIC CREAMY CORN CHOWDER

Ingredients:

2 cans (16 ounce) whole kernel corn, drained
2 to 3 medium potatoes, chopped
1 onion, chopped
½ teaspoon salt
pepper to taste
2 cups chicken broth
2 cups milk
¼ cup butter or margarine

Directions:

Combine first 6 ingredients in slow cooker. Cover and cook on low for 7 to 9 hours. Puree in a blender or food processor, if desired, then return to pot. Stir in milk and butter; cook on high about 1 hour more. Serves 6 to 8.

SLOW-COOKED SPINACH NOODLE CASSEROLE

Ingredients:

8 ounce dry spinach noodles
2 tablespoon. oil
1 ½ cups sour cream
1/3 cup all-purpose flour
1 ½ cups cottage cheese
4 green onions, minced
2 tsp. Worcestershire sauce
1 dash hot pepper sauce
2 tsp. garlic salt

Directions:

Cook noodles in a pot of salted, boiling water until just tender. Drain and rinse with cold water. Toss with oil. Combine sour cream and flour in a large bowl, mixing well. Stir in cottage cheese, green onions, Worcestershire sauce, hot pepper sauce and garlic salt. Fold noodles into mixture until well combined. Generously grease the inside of a slow cooker and pour in noodle mixture. Cover and cook on high for 1 ½ to 2 hours. Makes about 5 servings.

QUICK-PREP POTATO ONION SOUP

Ingredients:

6-8 potatoes, chunked
2 med. carrots, cubed
2 stalks celery, cubed
1 med. onion, chopped
1 tablespoon. parsley flakes
5 c. water
Salt and pepper to taste

Directions:

Cook in slow cooker on low for 8 hours or until vegetables are done. One hour before serving, add one can of evaporated milk.

VEGGIE LOVER'S CASSEROLE

Ingredients:

2 cups carrots, cut in strips, cooked & drained
2 cups celery, diced
1 onion, diced
¼ cup green pepper, diced
1 pint tomato juice
4 cups green beans, drained
1 teaspoon salt
dash of pepper
3 tablespoon tapioca
1 tablespoon xylitol or some stevia if desired

Directions:

Mix all ingredients together in slow cooker/slow cooker. Dot with 2 tablespoons margarine and cook on low for 8-10 hour or on high for 4-5 hours.

SLOW COOKED SPAGHETTI SQUASH

Ingredients:

2 c water
1 spaghetti squash, a size which will fit in a slow cooker

Directions:

With a skewer or large fork, puncture several holes in the squash. Pour water in the slow cooker, add the whole squash. Cover and cook on low for 8 to 9 hours. Split and remove seeds, then transfer the "spaghetti" strands to a bowl. Serve tossed with butter and salt and pepper, Parmesan cheese or your favorite sauce.

VEGGIE LOVER'S CURRY

Ingredients:

4 medium carrots, bias sliced into inch slices
2 medium potatoes, cut into 1/2 cubes
5 ounce can garbanzo beans, drained
8 ounce green beans, cut into 1 pieces
1 cup coarsely chopped onion
3 to 4 cloves Garlic, minced
2 tablespoon quick-cooking tapioca
2 tsp curry powder
1 tsp ground coriander
½ tsp crushed red pepper (optional)
¼ tsp salt
1/8 teaspoon Ground cinnamon
14 ounce Can vegetable broth
16 ounce Can tomatoes, cut up
2 cups Hot cooked rice
 Directions:

In a 3½ 4, or 5 quart crockery cooker combine carrots, garbanzo beans, potatoes, green beans, onion, garlic, tapioca, curry powder, coriander, red pepper (if desired), salt, and cinnamon.
Pour broth over all.
Cover; cook on low-heat setting for 8 to 10 hours or on high-heat setting for 4 to 5 hours.
Stir in tomatoes.
Cover; let stand 5 minutes.
Serve with cooked rice.
Makes 4 servings.

VEGGIE LOVER'S PASTA

Ingredients:

2 tablespoon butter or margarine
1 zucchini, 1/4" slice
1 yellow squash, 1/4" slice
2 carrots, thinly sliced
1½ cups mushrooms, fresh, sliced
1 package broccoli, frozen, cuts
4 green onions, sliced
2 to 3 cloves garlic, minced
½ teaspoon basil, dried
¼ tsp salt
½ tsp pepper
1 cup parmesan cheese, grated
12 ounce Fettuccine
1 cup mozzarella cheese shredded
1 cup cream
2 egg yolks

Directions:

Rub crock wall with butter. Put zucchini, yellow squash, carrots, mushrooms, broccoli, onions, garlic, seasonings and parmesan in the slow cooker. Cover; cook on High 2 hours. Cook fettuccine according to package directions; drain. Add cooked fettuccine, mozzarella, cream and egg yolks. Stir to blend well. Allow to heat for 15 to 30 minutes. For serving turn to Low for up to 30 minutes. Serves 6.

PARMESAN ZUCCHINI CASSEROLE

Ingredients:

1 red onion, sliced
1 green pepper, cut in thin strips
4 med. zucchini, sliced & unpeeled
1 (16 ounce) can diced tomatoes, undrained
1 tsp. salt
½ tsp. pepper
½ tsp. basil
1 tablespoon. butter
¼ c. grated parmesan cheese

Directions:

Combine all ingredients, except oil and cheese, in a slow cooker. Set temperature on low and heat for 3 hours. Dot casserole with oleo and sprinkle with cheese. Cook 1½ hours more on low setting. Makes 6 servings.

VEGGIES ITALIANO

Ingredients:

1 tsp salt
1 med eggplant, cut in 1" cubes
2 to 3 medium zucchini, halved & sliced ½"
1 large onion, sliced thinly
12 ounce fresh mushrooms, sliced
1 tablespoon olive oil
4 plum tomatoes, sliced ¼" thick
1½ cups mozzarella cheese, shredded
2 cups tomato sauce
1 tsp oregano
salt and pepper, to taste

Directions:

Toss eggplant and zucchini with the 1 teaspoon of salt. Place in a large colander over a bowl to drain for about 1 hour. Drain and squeeze excess moisture out. In a large skillet over medium heat, sauté onion, eggplant, zucchini, and mushrooms until slightly tender.

In the slow cooker, layer 1/3 of the vegetables (including sliced tomatoes), 1/3 of the the tomato sauce. and 1/3 of the cheese. Sprinkle with oregano, salt and pepper. Repeat layering 2 more times. Cover and cook on low 6 to 8 hours. Serve over rice, pasta, or other grain. Serves 6.

Slow Cooker

Miscellaneous

SLOW-COOKED ONION MUSHROOM BARLEY

Ingredients:

1 cup barley
1 can (14 ½ ounce) roasted garlic chicken broth (about 2 cups)
3 green onions, thinly sliced (about ½ cup)
4 to 6 ounces fresh or canned mushrooms, sliced
salt or seasoned salt and pepper to taste
2 teaspoons butter or margarine

Directions:

Combine all ingredients in slow cooker. Cover and cook on low for 4 to 4 ½ hours. You can leave out the barley, add vegetable broth and fresh garlic and milk of choice to make a mushroom soup – useful for other slow cooker recipes.

SLOW COOKER SWISS FONDUE

Ingredients:

1 clove garlic
2 ½ cups dry white Rhine, Chablis or Riesling wine
1 tablespoon lemon juice
1 lb. Swiss cheese, grated
½ lb. Cheddar cheese, grated
3 tablespoon flour
3 tablespoon kirsch
freshly ground nutmeg
pepper
paprika
1 loaf Italian or French bread, cut into 1-inch cubes

Directions:

Rub an enameled or stainless steel pan with garlic clove. Heat wine to a slow simmer (just under boiling). Add lemon juice. Combine cheeses and flour and gradually stir in. Using a figure-8 motion, stir constantly until cheese is melted. Pour into lightly greased slow cooker. Add kirsch. Stir well. Sprinkle with nutmeg, pepper and paprika. Cover and cook on high setting for 30 minutes, then turn to low setting for 2 to 5 hours. Keep on Low setting while serving. Using fondue forks, dip bread cubes into fondue.

SLOW-COOKED CHEESE & MACARONI MEAL

Ingredients:

8 ounce elbow macaroni, cooked and drained
4 c. (16 ounces) shredded sharp Cheddar Cheese
1 can (12 ounces) evaporated milk
1 ½ cups milk
2 eggs
1 teaspoon salt
½ teaspoon black pepper

Directions:

Place the cooked macaroni in greased slow cooker. Add the remaining ingredients, all except 1 cup of the cheese and mix well. Sprinkle with the remaining 1 cup of cheese and then cover and cook on low setting for 5 to 6 hours or until the mixture is firm and golden around the edges. Do not remove the cover or stir until it has finished cooking.

EGG-FREE MAC & CHEESE

Ingredients:

1 (16 ounce) pkg. macaroni, cooked & drained
1 tablespoon. salad oil
1 (13 ounce) can evaporated milk
1 ½ c. milk
1 tsp. salt
3 c. shredded sharp cheddar cheese
½ c. melted butter

Directions:

Lightly grease slow cooker. Toss macaroni and oil. Add all remaining ingredients. Stir, cover and cook on low 3 to 4 hours, stirring occasionally.

SLOW-COOKED BAKED POTATOES

Ingredients:

As many jacket potatoes you can fit in the slow cooker
Olive oil

Directions:

Prick potatoes with fork and baste with olive oil so skins don't dry out. Fill slow cooker with potatoes.
Cover and cook on high 1-2 hours or low 3-4 hours. Do not add water. If the potatoes are left too long in the slow cooker they will change color meaning the sugars start to caramelize – they can still be eaten though.

SLOW COOKER BANANA BREAD

Ingredients:

1 x ¾ c. flour (gluten-free or other)
2 tsp baking powder
¼ tsp baking soda
½ tsp salt
1/3 c. shortening
2/3 c. sugar (natural alternatives or leave out)
2 eggs, well beaten
1 ½ c. banana, well mashed, overripe
½ c. walnuts, coarsely chopped

Directions:

Sift together flour, baking powder, baking soda and salt. With electric beater on low, fluff shortening in a small bowl, until soft and creamy. Add sugar gradually if using. Beat in eggs in a slow stream. With a fork, beat in 1/3 of the flour mixture, ½ the bananas another 1/3 of the flour mixture, the rest of the bananas then the last of the flour mixture.

Fold in walnuts. Turn into a greased and floured baking unit or a 2 ½ quart mold and cover. Place on a rack in slow cooker. Cover slow cooker, but prop the lid open with a toothpick or a twist of foil to let the excess steam escape. Cook on high for 4 to 6 hours. Cool on a rack for 10 minutes. Serve Warm.

HOMEMADE BANANA WALNUT BREAD

Ingredients:

1/3 c. shortening
½ c. natural xylitol sugar
2 eggs
¾ c. all purpose flour (you can use gluten-free like tapioca and gram flour)
1 tsp baking powder
½ tsp baking soda
½ tsp salt
1 c. mashed ripe bananas
½ c. chopped walnuts

Directions:

Cream together shortening and sugar. Add eggs and beat well. Sift dry ingredients. Add to creamed mixture alternately with banana, blending well after each addition. Stir in nuts. Pour into well-greased ceramic souffle dish. Cover with foil and tie a string tightly around it to keep foil down. Pour 2 cups hot water in slow-cooking pot. Place mold on rack or trivet in pot. Cover with slow cooker lid and cook on high 2 to 3 hours or until bread is done. Be sure not to check bread during the first 2 hours of cooking.

SLOW-COOKED CAJUN PECANS

Ingredients:

1 pound pecan halves
4 tablespoon butter, melted
1 tablespoon chili powder
1 tsp salt
1 tsp dried basil
1 tsp dried oregano
1 tsp dried thyme
½ tsp onion powder
¼ tsp garlic powder
¼ tsp cayenne pepper

Directions:

Combine all ingredients in slow cooker. Cover and cook on high for 15 minutes. Turn on low, uncovered, stirring occasionally for 2 hours. Transfer nuts to a baking sheet and cool completely.

CHUNKY CINNAMON-SEASONED APPLESAUCE

Ingredients:

8 to 10 large cooking apples, peeled, cored, and sliced or cut in chunks
½ cup water
1 tsp cinnamon
½ to 1 cup sugar

Directions:

Put ingredients in slow cooker. Cover. Cook on low 8 to 10 hours. (High: 3 to 4 hours.)
Serve warm. Add cream if desired.

GRANOLA & APPLE CINNAMON CASSEROLE

Ingredients:

4 medium-sized apples, peeled and sliced
¼ cup honey
1 tsp. cinnamon
2 tablespoon. butter, melted
2 cups granola cereal

Directions:

Place apples in slow cooker and mix in remaining ingredients. Cover and cook on low for 7-9 hours (overnight). Serve with milk.

CRANBERRY APPLESAUCE

Ingredients:

10-12 medium apples
1-2 c. cranberry juice
lemon juice -- use 1/4 to 1/2 lemon
2 tbs natural sweetener (xylitol or stevia)
1/4 to 1/2 cup dried cranberries

Directions:

Wash the apples and chop them up without peeling. Squeeze lemon juice over them as you cut them.
Put apples in slow cooker with cranberry juice use 1 cup if you want the applesauce thick, more if you want it thin. Stir in sugar to suit your taste. Let apples stew on low for 6-8 hours. About an hour or two before serving, stir in cranberries.

The applesauce is a very pretty pink and the cranberries & juice give it a nice zing. As you can see, the recipe is simple and forgiving, let the apples stew a little longer or a little less, the longer you stew them the mushier the applesauce will be. It warms up nicely, or you can eat it cold.

Slow Cooker Fish

SLOW-COOKED TOMATO & WHITE FISH

Ingredients:

4 x 6 ounce (150g) white fish steaks or fillets
1 x 14 ounce (400g) can organic peeled Italian plum tomatoes – chopped
1 tablespoon organic tomato purée
minced or grated garlic – 2 cloves
fresh ground black pepper
salt to taste
1 diced green pepper

Directions:

Turn the slow cooker onto low. Grease the inside. Stir the tomato purée into the chopped tomatoes, season and add the green pepper and garlic Put fish fillets in the bottom and pour over the tomato mixture. Leave to cook for 3 to 5 hours - 2 to 3 hours on high if you prefer.

ORANGE LEMON SEASONED FISH

Ingredients:
1 ½ lb. fish fillets
Salt and pepper to taste
1 med. onion, chopped
5 tablespoon. chopped parsley
4 tsp oil
2 tsp grated lemon rind
2 tsp grated orange rind
Orange and lemon slices

Directions:

Butter slow cooker and put salt and pepper on fish to taste. Then place fish in pot. Put onion, parsley and grated rinds and oil over fish. Cover and cook on low for 1½ hours. Serve garnished with orange and lemon slices.

Slow Cooker

Desserts

PORT WINE CRANAPPLE COMPOTE

Ingredients:

6 cooking apples, peeled, slice
1 cup fresh cranberries
1 cup sugar (xylitol)
½ teaspoons grated orange peel
½ cups water
¼ cups port wine
sour cream , (low fat)

Directions:

Arrange apple slices and cranberries in slow cooker. Sprinkle sugar over fruit. Add orange peel, water and wine. Stir to mix ingredients. Cover, cook on low 4-6 hours, until apples are tender. Serve warm fruits with the juices, topped with a dab of sour cream. Serves 6.

CLASSIC CRANAPPLE CRISP

Ingredients:

3 apples (Any kind - I personally like Gala)
1 cup cranberries
¾ cup xylitol sugar or normal brown sugar if you haven't got xylitol
1/3 cup rolled oats (quick cooking)
¼ tsp. salt
1 tsp. cinnamon
1/3 cup butter, softened

Directions:

Peel, core and slice apples. Place apple slices and cranberries in slow cooker. Mix remaining ingredients in separate bowl and sprinkle over top of apple and cranberries. Place 4 or 5 paper towels over the top of the slow cooker, place an object across the top of the slow cooker and set lid on top.
This allows the steam to escape. Turn slow cooker on high and cook for about 2 hours. Serves 4.

SLOW-COOKED CINNAMON APPLES

Ingredients:
6 lg. cooking apples
¾ c. orange juice
2 tsp. grated orange rind
1 tsp. lemon rind grated
¾ c. rose wine
¼ tsp. cinnamon
½ c. brown sugar optional – or xylitol or you could try honey
Whipped cream

Directions:

Remove core from apples and place in slow cooker. Combine all other ingredients except whipped cream. Pour over apples. Cover pot and cook on low for about 3½ hours or until apples are tender. Cool and serve with whipped cream.

HONEY & APPLE CINNAMON GRANOLA COBBLER

Ingredients:
4 medium-sized apples -- peeled and sliced
¼ cup honey
1 tsp cinnamon
2 tablespoons butter -- melted
2 cups granola cereal

Directions:

Place apples in slow cooker and mix in remaining ingredients. Cover and cook on low 7-9 hours (overnight) or on high 2-3 hours. Serve with milk. Yield: 4 servings

CARROT NUTMEG PUDDING

Ingredients:
4 large carrots, cooked and grated
1 small onion, grated
½ teaspoon salt
¼ teaspoon nutmeg
1 tablespoon sugar (xylitol or honey)
1 cup milk
3 eggs, beaten

Directions:

Mix together carrots, onion, salt, nutmeg, sugar, milk, and eggs. Pour into slow cooker and cook on high for 3-4 hours.

SLOW-COOKED CUSTARD

In a heavy medium saucepan combine three egg yolks, light cream, sugar and salt. Cook and stir over medium heat. Continue cooking until mixture coats a metal spoon. Remove from heat; cool at once by setting saucepan in a sink of ice water and stirring for 1-2 minutes. Stir in 1 ½ teaspoons vanilla.

Cover surface with clear plastic wrap. In small bowl combine raisins. Place cherries in another bowl.

Heat ¾ cup sherry till warm. Pour 2/3 cup sherry over cherries. Set aside. Cut bread into ½-inch cubes (about 9 cups).

In a bowl, fold bread into custard, until coated. Grease a 6 ½ cup tower mold (without tube). Drain raisins and cherries, reserving sherry. Arrange ¼ of cherries in bottom of the mold, sprinkle 1/3 cup raisins into the mold. Add ¼ of bread cube mixture. Sprinkle with 2 tablespoons reserved sherry. Repeat layers three times, arranging cherries and raisins near edges of the mold. Lightly press last layer with back of spoon.

Pour remaining reserved sherry over all. Cover mold tightly with foil. Set mold in cooker - for a 5-6qt cooker, pour 1½ cups water around mold (for a 3½ - 4 qt cooker use 1 cup water). Cover, cook on low 5½ hours or until pudding springs back when touched.

Meanwhile make the sherry sauce:

In a mixing bowl combine 2 egg yolks, powdered sugar, 2

tablespoons sherry and ¼ teaspoons vanilla.

In small bowl, beat whipping cream until small peaks form. Gently fold whip cream into egg yolk mixture. Cover and chill until serving time. Remove mold from cooker, let stand 10 minutes. Carefully un-mold to serving platter. Serve warm with sherry sauce. Serves 12.

Alternative:

Remove pudding from mold, cover and chill. To serve, return pudding to same mold. Cover with foil, place in cooker. Pour 1½ cup water around mold. Cover, cook on high for 1½ to 2 hours, or until warm. Let stand 10 minutes, un-mold and serve with sauce.

CLASSIC CHRISTMAS BREAD PUDDING

Ingredients:

17 slices whole wheat bread or use some white bread as well
3 egg yolks, beaten
1½ cups light cream
2/3 cup dark Raisins
1/3 cup whole candied red cherries, halved
¾ cup cream sherry
1 cup - water
2 egg yolks, beaten
¼ cup Powdered Sugar, sifted
2 tablespoons Cream Sherry
1/3 cup sugar or sweet alternative e.g., Stevia
dash salt
1 ½ teaspoons vanilla
2/3 cup golden raisins
¼ teaspoon vanilla
½ cup whipping cream

Directions:

Using a few paper towels, cover the slices of bread after cutting-off the crusts and let them sit overnight.
On a low heat setting, blend the following ingredients together in a medium sized pan:
- sugar
- cream
- 3 eggs (yolks only)
- salt

(Tip: Substitute the sugar for organic coconut palm sugar, agave syrup, or low-calorie xylitol.)
Keep on low heat while stirring.

Shut off the burner and carefully dip the pan into cool water after the ingredients are thoroughly blended.
Next, add raisins and vanilla to the mixture then transfer to another bowl.
Very slowly heat up the sherry, then drizzle over the cherries using a different bowl.
After dicing the bread slices into cubes, coat them well with the custard.
Completely grease the inside of a tower mold.
As you drain the cherries and raisins, save the sherry to make a sauce.
Using the tower mold, start forming layers in this order: cherries, raisins, bread mixture plus 2 Tbsps sherry; REPEAT (makes approximately 3 layers)

Push down the top layer and cover it with foil.
Place the tower mold into a slow cooker with a few inches of water. Cover and cook on low approximately 5½ hrs. The pudding is done if it feels springy to the touch.

While the pudding cooks, prepare the sauce using the left over sherry.
Mix the sugar (powdered), 2 Tbsps sherry, 2 egg yolks, and ¼ tsp vanilla in a mixing bowl. Blend well.
In another bowl, vigorously beat the whipping cream. It will be ready when small peaks appear.
Next, carefully blend the whip cream into the egg yolk concoction. Cover it and let it chill until you are ready to serve.

Take the mold out of the slow cooker and let it rest for about 10 minutes.

Gently remove contents from the mold and transfer to a serving tray. Drizzle with sherry sauce and serve it warm. Makes enough for 12 people.

Another option: Take the pudding out of the mold, cover it and let it chill. Before serving, return the pudding to the mold, use foil to cover and put in slow cooker. Fill with a few cups of water and cook for about 2 hours on high or until desired temp (warm). Let it rest and cool - about 10 minutes. Carefully remove from mold and couple with sherry sauce to serve.

OLD FASHIONED APPLESAUCE

Ingredients:

About 3 pounds apples, peeled, cored, and sliced
1/3 cup sugar (recommend - xylitol)
1 cinnamon stick
2 tablespoon lemon juice
nutmeg

Directions:

Put apples in cooker. Sprinkle with sugar. Add cinnamon stick. Sprinkle lemon juice on. Cover and cook on low for 6½ to 8 hours until apples form a thick sauce. Sprinkle with nutmeg to taste.

Conclusion

With the wide range of choices, I believe you will have fun cooking these dishes in a slow cooker. A slow cooker is a good investment because you will not only save on energy; you will also save yourself from stress. Buy one now.

Made in the USA
Lexington, KY
03 June 2017